UPROOTED

An Anthology on Gender and Illness

Edited by Megan Winkelman, Hayley Beckett, Megan Collins, and Liat Litwin

www.uprootedanthology.com

...

"Consider how common illness is, how tremendous
the spiritual change that it brings…what wastes and
deserts of the soul a slight attack of influenza brings to
view, what precipices and lawns sprinkled with bright
flowers a little rise of temperature reveals, what
ancient and obdurate oaks are uprooted in us by the
act of sickness…it becomes strange indeed that illness
has not taken its place with love and battle and
jealousy among the prime themes of literature."

Virginia Woolf, *On Being Ill*

Contents

Foreword

ADELE MOSS

The second time around, I put on a pair of imaginary goggles and someone else's shoes to reread *Uprooted: An Anthology on Gender and Illness*. The wisdom and importance of these personal essays was never in question. Instead, I wondered if through someone else's eyes, the editors' curatorship, a quiet but intentional framing, could feel so tangibly *like a caring embrace*—a literary sort of synesthesia. I'm telling you, it does. In the last few years, I've watched editors and long-time collaborators Megan Winkelman, Hayley Becket, Megan Collins and Liat Litwin hold each other through illness and cradle this project with the same care. I'm lucky enough to have had them in my corner too. So freaking lucky. Our friendship is not the origin story behind *Uprooted*, but a living framework of conversation and intimacy, felt at every level of this exquisite book.

Exquisite does not mean easy. I am drawn to the stories in *Uprooted* that are raw, broken-open and frightening. The truth of illness scares me. But the courage to make it known is inspiring. The artistry employed to craft language into full expressions of its complexity is dazzling. "I admit, something dark and desperate must lurk under this skull," writes contributor

Leah Givens. Yes. Yes. Dear God, *I know*. These writers are hungry for truth-telling, and not in that angry, online, banal way. Their articulations are precise and bold. Forget the internet message boards, where I hold my hands in front of my eyes, only to peek through my fingers and glimpse the horror movie with sick fascination. Indulge in this embrace. Good art, like good friends, is essential.

Since college I've been working as a birthing doula, and within our culture, birth is ground zero for artificial gender and illness constructs. My job is to help my clients see their pain as neither senseless nor impossible. Their pain does not indicate an illness, injury or trauma. Their pain is not a slow death—it is quite the opposite. And when my clients relax into this realization, trust in their bodies' total capacity, when they surrender to the radical notion that their enormous pain is *okay*, they thrive in a miracle of fortitude and purpose—they give birth. It's wonder at their strength that keeps me struggling through a medical system that presumes immutable gender and sexual identities, that lists "pregnancy" as the "diagnosis of present illness," equating fertility with disease. My clients know about my wonder.

What they don't know is that I live with my own pain. Unlike pain in the birth process, which is at some point, finally, finally over, my pain continues. The word "chronic" sickens me and when I use it to describe my condition, I regret it immediately. Chronic? I refuse. This pain will end. It just hasn't happened yet. I am saying courageous things that I can't always believe. I am writing my first words about pain. I feel clumsy, writing as though for the first time.

"You talk about your pain all the time, *don't you?*" said one doctor. The more I verbalize it, she informed me, the more I make it real. So I've lived in fear of over-sharing, of real-making. I don't want to be like the girl in my cabin at summer camp who told us the exact same story of her mother's death every night. I tend to think I am that girl, that everyone braces themselves when I open my mouth. But my closest friends have reminded me that I actually talk about pain very rarely. In fact, I have also been criticized for under-sharing, for being weirdly mysterious about weekly appointments and invisible disabilities.

In a culture that would rather we cake our indecorums in the kind of makeup that doesn't quite match our skin tones, how do we talk about gender and illness? *Uprooted* has given me wise teachers. "The secrecy and loneliness is exhausting," writes Andrea Freund in her essay "My #RealResume." "When I started my blog," she begins, "I imagined the day that I'd be writing this post: a heart-warming retrospective about how I *used to be*." Instead, she's brave enough to reveal her eating disorder *now*, in all its ongoing ugliness. In her company, I realize it is not my own cowardice, shame or unique neurosis that prevents me from telling my story. *Uprooted* affirms the voices of those who have been told that their pain is their fault, that their caretaking duties must be selfless, that they should be skinnier, whiter, happier, more gender conforming, more alive. I have gained perspective on the system that has silenced me.

Uprooted dances between internal and external worlds. On the one hand, it celebrates language, expressivity and individual narrative as an authoritative source. There's no data or statistical modeling here, only human spirit. On the other hand, these writers respond to forces outside the self—the social constructs of gender and illness that largely predetermine our collective beliefs, behaviors and experiences. What a hot, charged line to tow.

Several essays detail the strange blurring of boundaries between the illness experience that you own, and one that is defined by forces outside your control. In Cathleen Calbert's "How to Be a Wife" we hear the mass echo of those voices. "Has he tried. Get him to try. Tell him he should try." Suddenly everyone's an expert. But when they see the illness up close, it offends them. "He's broken: he needs to be fixed! That he remains unwell seems absurd, obstinate, un-American." But it's the interaction of illness and the outside world that is absurd. Joan Annsfire's essay, as meandering and charming as a child, full of a bizarre and beautiful hope on the eve of surgery, puts it this way: "Strangers start conversations with me wherever I go. I sense I am giving off a new type of energy." Can I harness that new energy too?

I am not in chronic pain. I am in the process of birthing, slowly and painfully. Sometimes, when I'm patient and brave, I remember that Chinese medicine does not consider illness a problem. Instead, it is the body's way of pushing through something *to reach another side*. I'm not saying that everything happens for a reason, because I literally want to puke every time anyone says that. But when life is awful, we might as well make meaning out of its rubble. "I set out alone in the darkness on a gravel mountain road deep in the coastal forest," writes Gina Williams, my new teacher.

> I floated through the night in that rhythm, landing softly, relaxing into my stride, suspended in that perfect place where time becomes itself, where getting somewhere no longer matters.
>
> I pictured my dad at home as I ran, dozing in his chair in front of the television

or maybe in bed hooked up to his apnea
machine, his lungs laboring against the
weight of his enormous belly. I imagined
then that I could breathe for him, that the air
in my lungs became his […]

Yes, Gina, yes. I'm trying too. Make your lungs his
lungs. Make your fear into your longing, your strength,
your birth. Thank you, teacher, for the scary suffering
you've seen, and the magic and the meaning you have
created. Thank you, dear friends, for the gift.

Introduction

The story of this book, how it came to be and why, is inseparable from the story of our friendship.

Three years ago, one of us got sick. She felt like her identity—who she thought she was as a woman, sister, daughter, partner, and friend—had been destabilized. It seemed that the worlds around her were expanding, with graduations and new jobs and new cities, while chronic pain and fatigue were shrinking her own world to fit inside her bedroom walls. She wanted to hide, even from us, her best friends, but the disease progressed and hiding took energy she didn't have.

She began to talk to us, on the phone or in person. When she couldn't climb out of bed, we piled in next to her just as we had at our sleepovers, age six, twelve, twenty. She shared her strange new life, and we in turn articulated our own confusion and fear. Together we voiced our most vital stories: One of us lives with chronic illness, one of us cares for a sick parent; one of us is a rape survivor; one of us has watched relatives trapped in a state between life and death. We had known and loved each other for most of our lives, yet we were still learning to be fully vulnerable.

Within the small circle of our friendship, we began to question the way we had been taught to see our bodies and our health. We reviewed our experiences with fresh eyes, integrating our four stories and reconstructing their meaning. We talked about being women, our bodies living up to our expectations, and about living up to the expectations of others. While much remained unclear, it seemed that identity politics, especially around gender and sexuality, were invisibly regulating our lived understanding of health, and that troubled us.

The leap from having these conversations to deciding to make a book felt natural, so much so that we can't remember exactly how it happened. Our love of books led us to run our high school newspaper together, which was the first time we worked as a team of editors. Books were our first companions and our favorite teachers. Books were what we took to bed. They were what we took to waiting rooms. To the bathtub, to the hospital. Books have the power to transport the mind to places the body cannot go, to connect and unite a disparate audience.

On a visceral level we also knew that when the mind or body is in flux, it feels important to create something permanent, something constant. Pages won't change on you if you need a break. They can be re-read if brain fog or pain detracts from the first read. There is no need to be awake or asleep at regulated times, as with online forums or in-person discussions. An anthology in particular allows the reader to easily "dip in" and "dip out," making the content more accessible for those whose time and concentration is limited. The work of collecting, evaluating, and formatting is done for the reader.

This anthology became our way to develop an accessible dialogue among artists with very different personal experiences who were working to understand identity in illness. In 2014 we put out a call for submissions responding to the theme of "gender and illness." We gained twenty-seven incredible teachers who have collectively informed, and in many cases reshaped, our understanding of this theme. We learned that patient narratives cannot only be about the "illness" within the body, the struggle to fix and heal what is broken in flesh, blood, and bone. Patient narratives are always tethered to the living conditions and social structures that surround and construct illness, and the tension between the desire to heal and the push to redefine what needs to be healed. In this sense we see *Uprooted*'s content as more than personal, but also as political.

At the same time, personal narratives are also just that—a window into an individual's private experiences. *Uprooted*'s writers describe what it is like to mysteriously lose muscular functions after coming to terms with a sexual trauma; to slip into the depths of suicidal ideation during the final stages of a pregnancy; and to make public an eating disorder that has resulted from years of internalized pressure to look, act and eat a certain way. We learned what it feels like to go home to a partner with a new, terrifying diagnosis, and to begin the messy process of redefining partnership roles. We talk about death. We try to live on after death.

To "curate" means to take charge of and organize art—an essential process for an anthology. It also means to "take care of" more broadly, and if you do a quick search for synonyms you will find words like "warden," "archivist," "protector," "restorer," "guardian," "defender," and "keeper." Each of these words captures a different aspect of our collaborative, multi-year editorial process. We are curators—people who have assembled different stories, perspectives, and writing styles, who have organized them into a single showcase, and who feel fiercely the weight of our role as keepers.

In the content to follow we choose not to delineate based on theme, disease, or medium, though the order of essays, poetry, and fiction follows a loose narrative arc. We hope you will approach the collection as a living document, something to be shared, compared, countered, revisited, and reconciled. Our writers are old and young and from around the country and the world. They are teachers and nurses, professors and librarians. They are mushers, Scrabble players, roller derby blockers, and wildfire fighters. They have given you a part of themselves.

Where We Are
KAREN LAND

If someone told me you were alive, waiting a million miles away from this shell of a house—your home— where I now cower and sob alone, I would say, *Point me in the right direction.* And if the only way to get to you meant walking in the black of night, through dense forests, over mountains, across frozen seas, I would rejoice because there would be hope. Endurance is the one thing I understand, the only thing I trust. I would travel fast, my burdens light. You'd know that I was on my way, that I don't give up, that I never stop.

Do you rest at the edge of the ocean or stand on top of a summit? Which way do I go? Endurance means nothing without a compass. Endurance is pointless without you there waiting for me.

. . .

Two hundred middle schoolers fill the bleachers of a gymnasium near my parents' home in Indianapolis. These children know all of the answers. They usually do. "How long is the Iditarod Sled Dog Race?" I ask my audience. "Eleven hundred miles," the students say together. "How many dogs are on my team?" I remind them to raise their hands and point to a girl in all pink, perched on the top row of the bleachers. "Sixteen dogs!" she yells over the crowd, and then giggles. "And how long will it take us to run from Anchorage to Nome?" In every group, there is a comedian, a wise guy. "Do you mean how long it will take *you* or how long it will take the winners?" a boy with horn-rimmed glasses asks me from the front row. "That's a good question…" I start to respond when a teacher stands up, interrupting me. "Remember, boys and girls, that just finishing the Iditarod is a huge accomplishment. It's just as good as winning." *It's $50,000 less than as good as winning*, I think to myself, although I've never been in it for the money. No musher is. The boy with horn-rimmed glasses blurts out, "More people have made it to the top of Everest than across the Iditarod Trail by dog team." I tell the kid he makes a good point. He gives me a thumbs up.

Mom usually sits in the bleachers with the students, but now the wood is too hard for her bony body. The principal rolled a cushioned chair from the lounge down the hallway and onto the basketball court just for her. Sweat rolls down the skin under my shirt (it has to be one hundred degrees in here), but Mom, looking like a tiny bird in a huge nest, trembles. I pull the Iditarod parka from my bag of tricks—at the end of my talk I always dress up a student or teacher in a dozen layers of arctic clothing—and wrap it around her shoulders. A fleece stocking cap already covers her bald head. "I'm fine," she whispers to me and smiles. "Borage is taking care of me." My eleven-year-old Alaskan Husky, the real star of my Iditarod presentations, sits next to her and rests his big head in her lap. I continue my talk.

Ice…they want to know if I have ever fallen through the ice. People are fascinated by the idea that at any moment solid ground can shatter, give way, disappear below your feet. It makes me sick to think about it, let alone talk about it, but humans in a stifling hot gymnasium feel immune. They think it will never happen to them. Ice stories are only good stories if they have a happy ending, and obviously I am alive to tell one, so I do.

. . .

Rainy Pass was the highest point on the Iditarod Trail at 3,160 feet above sea level. We started the race in Anchorage at just above sea level and soon after began the long climb up the Alaskan Range toward Rainy Pass. What goes up must come down. A freefall descent down a narrow, rocky chasm called the Dalzell Gorge was a musher's only option to get to the next checkpoint. The drops in the Gorge were so drastic, so long, that it was all I could do to keep my sled from running over the wheel dogs directly in front of me. On my first Iditarod, I slammed my sled into a tree and flipped over at the top of the Gorge, dragging facedown in the snow behind my team for the entire plunge down the canyon. This time, on my second encounter with the Gorge, I didn't dump the sled once. *I've got this all figured out,* I thought.

The trail leveled off and I steered the sled wide just as my team wound like a snake around a tight U-curve. The night was black. I squinted, trying to make out what was happening; the narrow white beam of light coming from my headlamp barely illuminated my forty-foot-long string of dogs. I didn't realize we were running on ice, a frozen river, until the middle of my dog team— whoosh!—disappeared. I jumped on the brakes, slamming my two snowhooks into the packed trail to restrain my sled and team, and stumbled up the line. I reached out to feel the dogs still standing on the ice and counted as I moved forward: *two dogs, four dogs, six dogs, no dogs.* I looked down and saw nothing but more black and clouds of steam rising from a hole in the ice. I fell to my belly, lying flat out, and looked down over the edge.

That's when I saw them—Pepper, Cherry, Harp, Fir, Mohawk, and Bandit—swimming in place, all of them looking up at me. I reached down as far as I could, but a three-foot gap of air between the shelf ice and the surface of the water divided us. At one point, I grabbed Cherry by the collar and fumbled at her snap, trying to release her from the rest of the group so I could lift her to safety. But Cherry's snap, like all of their snaps, was frozen shut. It was a problem that had actually saved her life…all of their lives. Because the six dogs in the water were still bound together by the gangline and were also tied to their ten teammates standing on top of the ice, they weren't going anywhere. If I had succeeded in separating Cherry from the team, and if my numb hand had lost hold of her collar before I could pull her from the river, Cherry would have been gone, washed away with the current under a deadly roof of ice.

I slid back from the edge and sat up on my knees to think for a second. *There is no way I can pull six dogs out of this hole.* And then I did something really stupid. I crawled back up to the gap, swung my legs around, and jumped in feet first. I screamed out in shock. I was standing in fast moving water up to my waist. *This is suicide.* I had no plan. I just knew I needed a different angle on things and I wanted to be with my dogs. Right when they saw me land, their eyes lit up. They stared at me, astonished. *I don't know what to do,* I realized. But they did. Suddenly, I felt something tug on my parka. Instinct took over: when the dogs saw me, they saw a *ladder.* Pepper, my big red dog, climbed up my back, onto my shoulders, and used my head as his final step to freedom. The other dogs followed, scrambling and clawing their way up my body until it was just me down in that void, standing in the dark with water rushing all around me. *Alone*. But then I heard a whimper. I looked up and saw Pepper crouching over the edge, his head dropped low, his long nose reaching down to me like an open hand. I grabbed him by the neck and he, along with the rest of my team, pulled me up, out of the grave, and back to life.

. . .

"I could never do that..." the students and teachers mutter to each other. "Weren't you scared?" the boy with horn-rimmed glasses asks me. I look over at Mom swaddled in my parka, Borage's head still nestled in her lap, and her beautiful smile stabs me. *I'm always scared,* I think but do not say.

. . .

We are 1,800 miles apart, yet I am paralyzed by the blood. You, my sweet mother, describe the situation in detail over the phone. I drop to the kitchen floor and put my head between my knees, phone to my ear, listening. "I sat down on the couch after mowing the lawn and it happened. Blood between my thighs, blood all over the cushions, my pants drenched in it...blood on the carpet around my feet, my white socks...red, leaving a trail of footprints as Dad walked me out to the car."

I am no longer your daughter. Before this moment, you never would have given me—the sensitive one who passes out every single time a needle goes into my arm— such a gruesome account. My mother would have protected me from the ugly, the sad, the scary. But now you are different. All of that blood rushing from your womb altered you. Altered us. You are the child sitting alone in the darkness, your voice quivering over the thin telephone line connecting us—you in Indiana, me in Montana. I want to hold you. "Everything will be okay."

I don't know what else to say. "You will be fine." We don't speak the words, but we both know that this conversation, and all of that blood, is the beginning of our sad ending.

. . .

They send you home from the ER with a schedule of doctors' appointments for the week. A nurse recommends that you buy maternity pads and adult diapers to help contain the river of blood still streaming from your seventy-one-year-old body. You wait in the car for an hour while Dad paces the aisles of CVS, the same store where he once worked as a pharmacist, trying to find your supplies. I cry all night. My friend PJ stays with me, feeds my dogs and takes them outside, makes soup, tells me she understands. I hate her for trying to enter my grief, yet I know she's been here before. Just two years ago, her partner, only twenty-eight years old, died suddenly. You tell me not to come home yet: "Let's wait and see what the doctors say." But I ignore you. "I'm driving," PJ insists. I can't stop crying for long enough to argue with her.

. . .

I sit in the passenger seat of my own car. Waking from a nap, I remember with dread what is happening, where I am going. I do not open my eyes. Have I been sleeping for minutes or for hours? I know nothing. A soft rain tip-taps on the metal roof; *we must have driven straight through those storms,* I think. Chloe, my Corgi-Springer mix, drapes her chunky body across my lap. I feel her ribcage rising and falling with the breaths of animal sleep. I stroke her slick coat. She groans. She stretches. "Look," a voice, PJ, urges. I open my eyes. Chloe sits up. My other dogs, Borage and Jigs, both yawn and stand. Together, we witness a line of thick white steam rising up from the pavement, extending for miles from us to the far horizon. The long trail of silvery fog slices the green prairielands of South Dakota into perfect halves. The beauty reminds me that where we are is where we should be. For a moment, I feel peace.

. . .

Home. I get out of the car, let Borage and Chloe and Jigs out in the backyard, and then, like magic, the garage door begins to open. You are not expecting me, yet there you are. Your polished white sneakers appear first, then your ironed blue jeans, your navy sweatshirt decorated with flowers and Labrador Retriever puppies. You clap your hands like a little girl. Your face, revealed last, beams...round, smiling, joyful. "I knew you'd come home."

. . .

The lingering effects of anesthesia from your total hysterectomy and tumor debulking inspire strange questions. "When I die, where will you visit me?" you ask from a hospital bed in the recovery room. The question terrifies me, but my reply is quick. "Everywhere," I answer. "I'll go anywhere for you." You smile. "I know..." you say, your voice fading as you drift into sleep. "You'll find me."

Six Chanticleer Pears on NE 27th

TRICIA KNOLL

Yesterday I drove by those Chanticleers
in front of that brown bungalow
—my home for twenty years,
and that many since I left.
Chanticleers, good street trees
for an old neighborhood, stand three stories,
hacked open mid-canopy for power lines,
with ice-torn limbs and truck-scrape tattoos
—they stood up to bloom this sultry April,
white, fairy-teacup blossoms
drifting where the yellow tulips rise.

I saw how they've been tested,
blooms mounding in dry wind,
shriveled, ornamental, not fruitful
anymore.

On a warm spring planting day,
I had no placentas to line the holes
for those champagne-flutes of pear trees.
We tucked each in with one poem
layered below the root ball, an old sestet
about those who plant a tree

never knowing who lives the longest.

My hysterectomy trees I called them then,
planting grief for a lost womb, cajoling
a young couple and the ex-cop,
to join in to bloom, shade, and revive
our sun-fried, freeze-dried street.

The Cruelest Month
LEAH GIVENS

Winter whimpers; spring insists. April's unsettled atmosphere comes with blistering sun and warring tensions in my head. The wind outside is unsatisfied, a wash of whistles calling no one home. Birds settle in like sleepy children as the sun sings its own elegy.

I'm distanced from this cycle of life, window glass between me and the world. I haven't been outside today. For some people that's heresy. No work, no walk, no class, no coffee shop. My muscles don't appreciate giving in to laxity as the hours pass. My skin shivers and begs to bask. But my eyes, my eyes say: stay away from that abusive light. The source of all life is the source of pain. Night brings comfort, the robins' kind, the covers pulled up over welcoming eyes.

It sprouts in a spot above my right eye, a slight swelling of tissue that might not be visible to anyone but me. My fingers search and press instinctively as though I were bleeding. Most often the ache guides me to the notch in bone hiding beneath my eyebrow. I've learned that a nerve courses through there, a narrow yet forceful river. One feeds each eye; my left lies calm most of the time, but even it can turn fierce, threatening its banks. By what mechanism, that's the question and debate.

I spent years in medical school and started a neurology residency, but as a patient I'm barely better off. Science offers little more than educated guesses about the how and why of migraines, and in the depths of wordless burning, even those dissolve. Pure pain pulls you back, long past making eloquent sense of things. To the era when true words were just feelings and a syllable had to do. You massage that spot, turgid and hot, and dream of a razor blade for a quick incision. *Goo.* Goo is what would be extruded. A blighted cousin of the ancient Greek humors. Not pus, nothing infectious, but some similarly dense substance, black like motor oil. *Melancholy.* "Maybe you're just depressed," one doctor told me long ago. "Pain and sadness often go together."

Could that be? I wanted to grow angry, righteous, deny it. But my medical record would have needed bottles of white-out—now a team of computer hackers—to scrub all mentions of antidepressants and psychiatrist visits. I admit, something dark and desperate must lurk under this skull. Yet I don't blame unhappiness for flashing white lights in my vision as I stood in a college bookstore, signaling the onset of my first migraine. Nor claim that tragedy liked to stow away in the breathless high of a nighttime jog, ready to manifest as three days of unremitting sickness and headache.

I suspect that doctor and I both sensed the truth is more complicated. Today's neurologists would scoff at talk of the body's humors, instead agreeing that neurotransmitters must be involved—a physiological reason for the overlap with mood. In their offices they proffer and titrate medications for depression and anxiety, among other non-specific treatments, to try to ease chronic migraine. Worst case, they may advise patients to attempt only a limited life, hoping less stress will mean relief. It's a trajectory I know too well: I've watched myself, as if in a dream, go from working eighty-hour weeks to part-time to the stagnant pond of full disability.

Once a doctor myself, I understand the expectation that modern medicine should cure—and if not cure, treat effectively—and if not treat, at least explain the origins of any illness. But when my own headache specialist admitted she didn't know the cause of my condition, while her words didn't allay my physical pain, they assured me of her honesty and soothed my conscience: "I don't know" isn't "it's your fault." When she determined that there was nothing else she could do for me, I was set free to become an amateur researcher of new treatments. My transition from active staff scientist to disabled meant an ironic loss, not only of paycheck and job, but of easy access to my med school library's database, information on the newest and best ways to treat my condition. Unable to find most full scientific articles online, I gathered and sifted through what I could, joined related Facebook groups, had online conversations with patients, and made car and plane trips to meet doctors and surgeons. Related unpaid duties of a full-time migraineur, I've found, include learning to challenge the notion that pain must equal sadness. And searching, searching for a life that, if not migraine-free, still holds meaning.

. . .

The next night inches through the blinds. The black tar is back, pooling in that same hollow. Mental messages stick and fail to transmit. Another night of no writing. I miss that mind-clearing hike, learning as I go and leaving a marker behind.

This time I refuse. To give in, to deepen my human-shaped crater in bed. Almost impossible now, without a pill or two. As I swallow, I'm grateful to medication for padding this brain-made stabbing. The drug calms the throbbing, but take it too often and headaches will boomerang, slapping back harder than before. Besides, the monthly medication limits of my doctor and insurance company leave me no way to tame each of my many migraines, not completely.

A muted whooshing in my head rises to displace the night's quiet. Again I open the window, hoping for a cool blanket of air. The cat races to the sill to listen for any fluttering feathers. Minutes pass before a siren flies by, an ambulance in the distance.

Today I did go outside. Once, in a break from the pain. Along the street neighbors played gardener and farmer in the comfortable sun. With the natural light my body remembered that the day does not begin and end with the flick of a switch.

That body flies to the toilet before I know it. *Not you; oh, yes, you.* Sudden unexpected vomit, the detested guest of migraine-brain. Lentils, not pretty. Ah, well. I'm better than I would be in the nineteenth century. *Survival of the fittest*; I shudder at the thought. Modern medicine has kept me living; I think that's a good thing. It's hard to remain convinced while my stomach threatens to expel the rest of dinner.

The night is black, closer to day, and no sleep of which to speak. But I know the cycle: an unplanned purge can loosen my head's taut net of pain almost immediately. Like a storm, growing then breaking, the migraine may begin to withdraw, though its clouds can linger for days.

As I lie down, testing the nausea, the cat bounds in beside me, licking my skin rapid-fire as if this is some great adventure. I pull the sheet over my head. *Not now.*

Plop, she flops near the edge of the bed, instantly exhausted. I peek out and laugh despite the ache. When you feel like dying, it's not always medicine that brings you back to life. And it is hardly ever medicine that gives you reason for living.

The Urge to Believe Is Stronger than Belief Itself

ERIN M. BERTRAM

~for my mother~

We hug as she steps into my brother's Jeep. The pressure of its passenger seat belt first alerted her to the discomfort in her chest. Our breasts touch, & I fix on the discarded bottle of gin lying mouth open & empty on the parkway.

I feel guilty for having breasts, ashamed of their substantial shape, their flagrant assertion of health. In three weeks, she will have one where a pair once stood heavy & proud. The doctors will consider her lucky. She will consider reconstruction as the vinyl bag is emptied every two to three hours.

My father lugs the easy chair upstairs into what used to be my room. This is where she spends her days, her nights. On the arms & where a tail might rest, the fabric's begun to wear, burgundy rubbed pale. Quietude trumps plentitude. On the television, platefuls of food. Her heart finds stasis. Mine beats & beats & beats.

Plural Form: -mies

Etymology: Greek *mastos* breast + English *-ectomy* removal

Definition: (*n*) the surgical removal of all or part of the breast, occasionally including the removal of associated lymph nodes &/or muscles of the chest

See Also: radical mastectomy, modified radical mastectomy, segmental mastectomy, simple mastectomy

It's only a part of her body, but it's a part of her body. We become acutely aware of the florid architecture at the cellular level. How one cell could be so greedy, leave nothing for the others, save those it recruits. How I instinctively put a full tank of gas in my car. How I buy beer. How her body is wrecked just enough to offer sanctity as the only possible answer—if she doesn't get better, what then?

How I sip St. Peter's, curse, open my lips in shocked prayer. How my brother calls & I barely recognize his baritenor. How her Multiple Sclerosis has suddenly vanished. How I collect portents, compulsively, or what I mistake for them: heat lightning, harvest moon, a family of possums living beneath the deck. How we clumsily compose litanies of *at least*s. How we try to exhume a sense of calm, of easy coolness, from within the storm's one wild eye.

Diagnosis vs. prognosis. Evanesce vs. convalesce. All a matter of index, of glossary. A matter of what merits a name & how it, then, is treated. Any change is worth noting.

Plural Form: -s

Etymology: Middle English *brest*, from Old English *breost*; akin to Old High German, Old Irish, Russian

Definition:

1. (*n*) a pair of curved protrusions in the female, consisting of mammary glands & concerned with the flow of milk

2. (*n*) the ventral part of the body between the neck & the abdomen

3. (*v*) to resist something hostile or threatening with courage & resolve

4. (*n*) the core of emotive activity

See Also: multipurpose objects, symptom of tenacity

Dear—

Paper rustling, cars backfiring at odd hours, the snap of the moon's wan neck against an unmoved sky. Forgive me my ether, this letter likely never sent. Forgive the time, at sixteen, I threw *fuck you* in your face.

Even now, years later, a teacher, a volunteer, a woman with short hair drawn to other women, I know I am not the daughter you had in mind. I know you love me, though, & fully. Are learning, daily, to love me more.

Love,

Self-Examination

Following your period (or the same time each month, if you do not get your period), check for any change in the normal look & feel of your breasts, i.e. dimpling, rash, puckering, nipple discharge, etc. Any change is worth noting.

In front of a mirror, in the shower, or lying down:

1. Use the pads of the three middle fingers on your right hand to examine your left breast.
2. Press using light, medium, & firm pressure, circularly, side to side, & up & down, respectively.
3. Feel for changes above & below your collarbone, & in your armpit area.
4. Use the pads of the three middle fingers on your left hand to examine your right breast.
5. Repeat steps 2 & 3.

My mother shifts her weight in the recliner. Another chocolate milkshake. The way we are bound by the solid frame of habit & every subtle crack.

Outside a café, her friend waits in the car. My mother's friend has forgotten my mother needs this week & the next two off, & so spends Tuesday morning sipping coffee by herself. Her breath clouds the windows with a legion of tiny water droplets. She switches the radio on, sings a verse or two of "Desperado." She sips her coffee by herself.

Did my mother's dog draw his small muzzle again & again above her belly? Did he fall asleep, night after night, against her finely tucked arms instead of the camber of her skinny legs? In stories, it's instinct that sniffs out the body's faults, that earnestly nuzzles that which is best, once removed, left alone. Her dog all coat & tail, paw both a noun & a verb, his small ears two earnest semaphores, waving her down with a message she didn't yet understand.

In my study: *Things Fall Apart, Heaven's Coast, Into The Wild, Traveling Mercies, Lives on the Boundary, Regarding the Pain of Others, No Accident, Sweet Machine, The Anchorage, Written on the Body, The Last Clear Narrative, Legitimate Dangers, Uncertain Grace.*

They say Bethesda was a pool dug to slake the thirst of roaming flocks. It's only when an angel, nimble as a gnat, swooped down & broke the water's seal with a blessing that, with one dip of the toes, the pool began to lift, from those who'd gathered there, the considerable weight of age & of disease. An underwater house of grace, its crowds awaited submersion with a faith anything but pliant. I choose to believe there are angels circling the deep.

Plural Form: -does or -dos

Etymology: Middle French *bravade* & Old Spanish *bravata,* from Old Italian, to challenge, show off from *bravo*

Definition: (*n*) a pretense of bravery, at times daft, foolhardy

See Also: they say each time God closes a door, another opens—God slams a door, forgets to lift a window & yet

First, MS, a misfire, one eye gone dark, the other pulling the weight of sight. Now a second errant bullet, cancer, this one lodged scattershot in her chest, in glands, in nodes, in ducts.

They began at 12 o'clock, radiated clockwise. Of four quadrants, squatters sat in two. The decision was made.

Parabola, crescendo, source of nourishment when I was young, putty tugged in the dark, assumed. Now, no breast where once one was. We are victims of symmetry, yes. Was she prepared to sever herself from herself?

Since the diagnosis, I've reached for a book every minute untethered. Poems, yes, with God grafted down their center, Christ bleeding in recto, in verso. Poems without God, too. The doves on the fire escape become homing pigeons, the stray cat a force scattered & pervasive. Prayer flags licking at the wind.

Dear—

Corn grays in its husk. The field before a field, the field after. Catfish darting through dirty current, blending & yet somehow not. Something always stands out when they flip the switch & the backdrop, even that, falls away. A table, maybe. A few stray sweaters slumped against the floorboard. Months pass, & one day the fallen colt, disappeared behind a neighbor's barn, dissolves into soil & peat.

We lived in the suburbs, removed from farm country, but I remember you telling me once, passing a farm along the highway, how we should appreciate the land & those who work it. Because our bodies comprise the very earth we walk on.

Love,

Note:

Cancer is not invasive like a virus or bacteria, an injury or a trauma. Cancer is a disease of the self. The body's own cells assume a guise & stage a quiet coup.

Breast cells, on average, take one hundred days to double. One billion cells form a tumor 1 cm in diameter. Which means most cancers have been around for six to ten years prior to diagnosis.

Post-mastectomy options include reconstruction (muscular— abdominal or thoracic; fatty tissue; saline/silicone implant— including or not including cadaver skin), prosthesis (cotton, plastic, rubber, or gel), no action.

Study for *Prière de Toucher (Please Touch)*.

Plaster cast. Nipple round as the bulb of a lemon, flat, shy, leaning into the fine curvature of the shadow it casts for itself, by itself. It just hangs there, matted in shadowbox, semisphere circumnavigated by lines & subsequent angles.

Museumgoers, though initially encouraged to touch the breast, are interrupted, mid-gesture, and kept from doing so. Interactive art rendered immobile. Study for *Prière de Toucher (Please Touch)* would be the only work to be placed behind glass & remain behind glass for the sake of the longevity of one plaster breast in a box.

Note:

Insurance plans may or may not offset the cost of prostheses. Federal law, however, requires reconstruction coverage, as surgery is assumed to once again render an individual whole.

Plural Form: -gies

Etymology: New Latin *pathologia* & Middle French *pathologie,* from Greek *pathologia* (study of the emotions), from *path-* + *-logia* -logy

Definition:

1. (*n*) the study of the essential nature of diseases, especially the structural & functional effects they produce

2. (*n*) something abnormal

See Also: matters of degree, not difference

Pathology Report

Early:

- *Stage 0 (carcinoma in situ)*
- *Stage I*
- *Stage IIA*
- *Stage IIB*

Advanced:

- *Stage IIIA*
- *Stage IIIB*
- *Stage IIIC*
- *Stage IV (metastasis)*

Technically, there are eight stages.

How could there be any more than two.

After the surgery, three medicines: one, twice daily, two taken at will. She requires, we enumerate: three knit blankets, a straw, socks at all times, more sleep than waking life. She gets to keep her hair. On the eighth day, the right shoulder is held 1.5 inches above the left on account of the saline expander leaning against a confused pectoral wall. At the hospital, at regular intervals, more salt water is added, slowly, painfully, eventually making room, inside her body, for a small, quiet ocean.

The dog, who had licked her face & neck furiously in the weeks leading up to the diagnosis, would not be shaken. He sat by her side, vigilant, entirely still, his small body, all ten pounds of him, in contact with her body as often as possible.

One billion breast cells form a tumor 1 cm in diameter. Jawbreaker. Chokecherry. Wad of crumpled paper. A finger of whiskey, cup filled a fifth of the way to the lip. Cup filled a fifth of the way. Cup spilled over.

Note:

Seven to ten days following surgery, patients may feel an overwhelming sensation that their body has not changed. This may result in overactivity, which has been known to cause exhilaration & extreme weakness.

This does not happen to her.

She is lethargic, quiet mostly, every movement, every word, slow & heavy. Deliberate. Unmistakable. Her energy, though diminished, is recognizable, though, familiar, even through the haze.

In addition to asking me to drain the saline bag, safely pinned to the elastic of her pajama bottoms, of its blood-tinged runoff, she asks me to lower her down into the bath.

My mother asks me to bathe her, gently. And I do it.

I do it with a gentleness I didn't know I had.

The urge to believe is stronger than belief itself.
The urge to believe is stronger than belief itself.
Any change is worth noting.

Nights I wake dry-mouthed. Naked. Blinking. Each time, a slight shift in feeling, as when someone enters a room filled with people talking, laughing, emptying drinks, filling them up again. And everyone takes notice.

In the air, the sour-sweet smell of hat-head. Of sandalwood, incense freshly snuffed. And the cool, metallic charge of a coming rain.

Dear—

But are you not, as you said, your body. Are they not, in their quiet heft, together, four percent your agile frame. I've done the math, twice.

One night, with my best friend, on a dare, I tugged one of mine from its cup, placed it on the postal scale on my desk. It rested there awkwardly, weighed 2.5 lbs. Once, I woke clutching them both, groping for a loophole, guilty for having & holding what you no longer possess.

I would give them to you if only I could. Birthday, Christmas, Mother's Day, whatever. I wonder, would you take them?

Love,

An absence of visual aid does not render an image silent.

Does it.

I imagine a place where all she is manages to be spur & accord & light.

The woman I was involved with at the time pours hot water over stones, places them at telling corners of my mother's body, & the steam rises, fills her lungs like camphor, like eucalyptus. My mother's nurse friend gifts her with massage, the quiet strength woven in her hands.

My brother leaves a bouquet of twenty-five open-mouthed orchids, a chorus of exquisite color. And my aunt brings cooking magazines, recipes a gesture to the future we will for her, despite the fear that's settled deep in our guts—silt at the bottom of a mile-wide river.

My mother: grateful, yet so still.

So still.

Behind her pectoral wall, an implant presses its body against & against her heart. Most days, the liquid stills. Others, the whorling muscle spasm, quaff of water & requisite pill. A small amount of saline is added every three to four weeks. The liquid presses & presses until its presence is made, finally, known.

When we found out the cancer was gone, that the doctors had done well with their shiny instruments, that she was, somehow, to be spared, I scrawled these words repeatedly in ink, in earnest:

A few hundred crows descending a field.

I would have counted them.

Would have kissed each one,

Bent my wet neck into each of theirs,

Muttered flutter, flutter

Notes

The title and phrase "the urge to believe is stronger than belief itself" is borrowed from Alix Olson's spoken word poem "[myth]."

The definitions are adapted from the *Merriam-Webster Dictionary*.

Gynecomastia

ASAD ALVI

Gynecomastia,
they scribble down
in the medical report—
the sole clinic in town—
Gy-ne-co-mas-tia,
on sheets of paper.
"Your son's got this,"
Dr. Dilbar and assistant
tell Zeena, my mother,
"a disorder, you see."
Gy-ne-co-mas-tia,
them, scribbling down.

I can scarce pronounce it,
Gy-ne-co-mas-tia,
but perhaps it is apt
that this swell should be
as inscrutable, disorderly
as all myself.
They should've called it
the falling of rain.

The rain was never discovered,

so no one would ever believe
my own theory
of my own disease:

For they say licking the tip of one's breast
can cause it to swell, grow,
became more prominent, so;
this body-bulge, once a molehill,
is the crest of a mountain now.
Zeena tells me 'tis a disease,
this growth behind my shirt.
I should see a doctor.
And sometimes, pauses,
asks, shivering,
"Where have you been?
You've not done something
bad, have you? No, No,
my boy cannot sin, my boy, good boy!"
The call from the mosques
bellows into the air,
takes hold of her; gnawed.
Her god's a brutal fraud.
So we are here, now,
the sole clinic in town.
The clinic of gods?
And *Gy-ne-co-mas-tia,*
Dr. Dilbar scribbles down.

Unaware.

Of the thousand other explanations
that breathe of indiscretions
behind unraised, dingy shades
that hid our kiss cascades,
those netted palisades:

The motel room was lit of rouge.
My boyfriend left incorrigible traces,
his tongue circling the periphery
of my chest.
My breasts are larger
than they are *supposed* to be.
Like a plant that was not to grow
any taller.
Or rain that was not meant
to fall more.

Dr. Dilbar, scribbling down,
mistaking the overflow
of rain for disease,
reduces the tenor
of undone sarongs,
the body-wrongs,
of maddened siren-songs
to an altered ratio
of estrogens and androgens:
Gy-ne-co-mas-tia,
them, scribbling down.

But I think I prefer it.
I should take it as something benign.
You see, we have a phrase in Pakistan:
Jo hoa achey k liye hoa!
Whatever's done is done for good!
We inherited it from the gods.
Politicians use it to justify
the rigging throughout elections.
'Tis a capitalist mantra, too,
to keep the lowly man
lowlier so.

I never thought I would use it,
but sickness makes us blasé,
fatalistic.

I find my sickness beautiful now;
how consoling, when,
as Dr. Dilbar scribbled down,
the contortion on Zeena's face
retreated like a wave
that ebbs by noontide.
"It's only a disease,"
she breathed thus.
"My boy's picked rosaries
since childhood in mosques,
my boy, good boy!"

I am obscured before her,
and she smiles.

"Surgery,"
Dr. Dilbar says at last.
"Tomorrow. Five."
The concocting of rain
shall be undone.

I mourn
that its falling
won't wet her sleeves.

Tender Points
AMY BERKOWITZ

Δ

The Sphinx's riddle: What goes on four legs at dawn, two legs at noon, and three legs in the evening?

I don't particularly like riddles. But then again, neither did travelers passing through Thebes. They didn't try to solve the Sphinx's riddle because they craved the intellectual challenge. They tried to solve it because the Sphinx killed anyone who didn't.

I don't like riddles. And yet here I am, obsessed with solving a riddle of my own, the riddle of my body: Why, exactly, am I constantly in pain?

Like the Sphinx's riddle, mine is not a brainteaser. It's not Sudoku. It's not something you do on the bus to make the ride feel shorter. Like her riddle, mine has a greater urgency.

ΔΔ

In *The Culture of Pain*, David B. Morris criticizes medical literature for its tradition of approaching pain as a riddle to be answered, a challenge to be met, a puzzle to be solved. He rejects the language of conquest and asks us instead to consider regarding pain as a mystery.

While a puzzle can be solved with just one or two missing pieces, pain is much more complicated, and talking about pain—especially chronic pain—as if it has an easy answer can be irresponsibly deceptive. Morris suggests that by understanding pain as a mystery, we can respect its complexity and recognize the alienating experience of living in pain. "Mysteries," he writes, "introduce us to unusual states of being…. Mysteries disturb the world we take for granted."

ΔΔΔ

An invisible illness with uncertain causes and imprecise diagnostic criteria, fibromyalgia is largely defined by its mystery.

And yet, when the onset of this pain follows a traumatic event (as it often does), it's hard not to understand that trauma as a certain kind of key. To hold that key in a palm made sweaty by too much coffee. To never put it down for the feeling that at any moment, it could completely unlock the mystery and solve the problem of your pain.

ΔΔΔΔ

2 at the bottom of the neck just above the collarbone
2 just below the center of each collarbone
1 on the crease inside each elbow
2 more on the inside of each knee

On the back of the body, 2 at the bottom of the neck
1 above each shoulder blade and just inside each shoulder blade
2 on either side of the lower spine
2 more on the outer part of each hamstring
In order to be diagnosed, the patient must experience discomfort in at least eleven of eighteen tender points designated by the American College of Rheumatology.

△△△△△

I like Morris's idea of pain as something more complex and unknowable than a simple puzzle. And yet, when it comes to the mystery of my pain, I can't resist the impulse to solve it. I have all these pieces, and I can't stop my hands from wanting to jam them together until some sense emerges.

△△△△△△

When I think about my clues, they are inside a wicker basket that I'm carrying through the woods. It's nighttime. It's quiet. I realize that, for some reason, I am Little Red Riding Hood. Why? I should be thinking of Nancy Drew or Harriet the Spy. Some story about a girl detective, not about a girl waylaid in the woods.

But to solve this kind of mystery, it seems, you need to walk alone into a forest. You need to walk until you meet a wolf.

Throughout pop culture, Little Red Riding Hood's wolf is read as a sexual predator, from Sam the Sham's seductive canine to Susan Brownmiller's rapist.

I have a wolf in my story. But he will not interrupt my walk through the forest. Which is to say he's already interrupted it: he's the reason I'm here, sorting out the aftermath. Which is to say the wolf is eternally interrupting my walk through the forest: emerging from behind the same tree again and again to block my path. Imagine it repeating like a GIF.

My Little Red Riding Hood has no granny in the woods. She has no treats in her basket. Her basket is for gathering clues. A handful of fur or a whisker she yanks from his face. Could be DNA tested later.

ΔΔΔΔΔΔΔ

Riding my bike to the doctor's office in Fort Greene, I am aware of vibrations from the handlebars and how they make my wrists and hands tingle and go numb. The usual shoulder pain and a weakness in my hips, but I can ride my bike. It's a mild winter day in 2008 and I'm wearing a silk scarf around my neck to keep the wind off my skin.

I lock my bike outside and walk into the small office. The doctor asks about my pain. He presses my body in eighteen places. My back, my shoulders, legs, arms, neck. Where does it hurt. He walks into another room, I'll be right back. I hear a printer vibrate/buzz. He comes back with a sheet of paper: a diagram of a body with eighteen tender points. A diagnosis of fibromyalgia.

Fine with me. A great relief to have a name for this. I know the true name of this disease—My Body Is Haunted by a Certain Trauma—so I don't much care what other name it has, so long as it has one. Something to point to. Something to call it.

And later, yes, I get the blood work done. No Lyme, no lupus, no whatever else. Confirms the sloppy diagnosis of exclusion. Fine with me.

ΔΔΔΔΔΔΔ

A few years after I graduated from college with a degree in literature, I found myself working at the world's largest market research company. My job was analyzing consumer sentiment as expressed in online spaces. This was another way of saying that I spent eight hours a day lurking on message boards.

The company's biggest clients were pharmaceutical companies, which meant that the message boards I lurked on were message boards for people with cancer and other serious illnesses.

As you would expect, these messages, written by sick people and their caregivers, were intensely emotional.

I am so happy the scans were good! Healing hugs and blessings. <<<hugs>>> Hugs to you and yours. Love and hugs. Prayers and hugs. Take good care everyone! My prayers are with you. Keep us posted.

But the world's largest market research company was uninterested in emotion. What they had me looking for was sentiment: I scored each sample as positive, negative, neutral, unsure, or no opinion. People and their details were shucked away, unless they were significant enough to be included in the qualitative results.

My job was to leverage this data to identify key factors that would make sick and dying people more interested in purchasing very expensive medicine.

DH is on erbitux/oxaliplatin/5fu/leucovorin. He has the erbitux rash BAD, but onco is hesitant to prescribe an antibiotic.

It was while I was immersed in this culture of online illness, with its own language of acronyms and emoticons, that I got sick myself.

ΔΔΔΔΔΔΔΔ

Working hurt. The precise mousing of data entry made my wrists go numb, and sitting at the keyboard made my shoulder muscles spasm. On the worst days, the stiffness spread to my hips and legs. The doctor in Fort Greene wrote a letter recommending a two-week rest period.

I faxed his letter to the HR department of the world's largest market research company. I called and emailed and they didn't answer. I left messages that they didn't return. I applied for short-term disability, and my claim was rejected twice.

When the two weeks were over, I didn't feel any better. The doctor recommended another week of rest. I faxed, emailed, called HR. I was met with the same radio silence, which was starting to sound an awful lot like a static crackle softly whispering *you lazy bitch we don't believe you're sick, trying to trick us, you worthless piece of shit.*

Coincidentally, I came back to work the same day as another analyst who had been out sick. He had broken his ankle snowboarding, and he was wearing a boot. His cubicle was decorated with get well soon cards, and an Edible Arrangement bloomed festive pineapple chunks next to his monitor.

My cube was as bare as I'd left it. A get well soon card would have acknowledged the fact of my illness, and as far as the world's largest market research company was concerned, I was faking it.

Picturing my cubicle next to my coworker's is a perfect illustration of Morris's distinction between male and female pain:

In *The Culture of Pain*, he writes: "Female pain is regularly disregarded, discounted, and dismissed, largely because it does not always conform to the clear organic model of appendicitis or a broken arm."

ΔΔΔΔΔΔΔΔΔ

The story of my pain is not an easy story to tell. And I'm not talking about the emotional difficulty of telling it; I mean the plot itself is confusing. Trauma is nonlinear. There are flashbacks and flash-forwards. And my story is a story about forgetting. Forgetting is one of the main characters; in fact, he may be the hero. Forgetting swoops down on a rope to rescue me right after my rape. He holds me with his free arm as we swing back to safety, saying, "You can't handle this right now, but you'll remember when you're twenty-three, and you'll have better psychological defenses then, and a good therapist."

If Forgetting is the hero of the story, who is Memory? And what happens to Memory in the end?

ΔΔΔΔΔΔΔΔΔΔ

There's a *This American Life* segment about a couple that's furnishing their new apartment. They buy a table on eBay at a very reasonable price. When it arrives, they realize they've accidentally ordered dollhouse furniture. The table is two-and-a-half inches, not two-and-a-half feet, tall. Smaller than most of the things they were planning to put on it.

This dollhouse table feels familiar.

My memory of that day is in miniature. Although it's very clear, it's about two-and-a-half inches tall and stuck inside my head. I can't show it to anybody. I can't locate a corresponding full-size memory out in the world. And I can't even tell you what day *that day* was.

ΔΔΔΔΔΔΔΔΔΔΔΔ

In 2012, somebody decided to figure out exactly which day Ice Cube's song "It Was a Good Day" was written about.

By analyzing the lyrics, Donovan Strain ultimately concluded that the only day when *Yo! MTV Raps* was on the air, the weather was clear and smogless in LA, beepers were commercially available, and the Lakers beat the SuperSonics was January 20, 1992.

I worry that I'm starting to fetishize this practice of resurrecting the past.

ΔΔΔΔΔΔΔΔΔΔΔΔΔ

Here is what I know: I first remember the rape thirteen years after it happened. The next morning, I wake up with pain all over my body. The pain is eventually diagnosed as fibromyalgia.

△△△△△△△△△△△△△

I keep having this vision of my body shot through with systems of hidden stairs and hallways—secret, steep, ill-maintained servants' quarters. Imagine that the stairs climb up my arm and neck and lead to doors in and out my ears, then back down the other arm. In these dim, drafty passages, memories creep through my body right next to present perceptions.

After the death of her husband, Sarah Winchester used her share of the Winchester rifle fortune to build a sprawling and peculiar mansion to appease the spirits of the vast number of people killed by her husband's rifles. Convinced that the spirits would murder her if she ever stopped construction, Sarah hired workers to build round the clock, so that the house was never complete. This continued for thirty-six years, until her death in 1922.

Many people with fibromyalgia experience non-restorative sleep; that is, no matter how long they sleep, they wake up feeling tired. Like many things about fibromyalgia, the cause of this sleep disorder is unknown. One theory is that the sympathetic nervous system's "fight or flight" response is constantly activated, increasing nocturnal vigilance and preventing restful sleep.

What vigil is my sympathetic nervous system keeping? It

seems to be supervising construction of a mansion designed to ward off evil spirits. It's building secret passages inside my body to route the past around the present and keep trauma out of sight, like servants in a smoothly running household.

ΔΔΔΔΔΔΔΔΔΔΔΔΔΔ

It's only when the pain is severe or when the pain prevents me from doing something that I'm forced to think about it. But even when I'm not thinking about it, it's still there. My body is riding BART and it's in pain. My body is peeling an orange and it's in pain. My body is worrying about something stupid and it's in pain. My body is writing this and it's in pain.

ΔΔΔΔΔΔΔΔΔΔΔΔΔΔ

I agree with Morris that chronic pain isn't a puzzle with an easy answer. But in the case of fibromyalgia pain in particular, it can be equally damaging to insist on its mysteriousness.

Fibromyalgia is routinely described in terms of its lack of certainty or credibility. Even the National Institute of Health website has a troublingly vague grasp of the illness: "The causes of fibromyalgia are unknown, but there are probably a number of factors involved."

Up to ninety percent of fibromyalgia patients are female, and there is a strong precedent for "women's voices not being heard or considered credible in the male-dominated health-care system," as noted in "The Girl Who Cried Pain," a study by Diane E. Hoffman and Anita J. Tarzian. While I can't say for certain how fibromyalgia would be discussed if the condition primarily affected men, I suspect that we would see words like "mysterious" and "unknown" drop from the literature, replaced by the findings—however incomplete—of research done thus far.

△△△△△△△△△△△△△△△△△

Because of this misogynistic insistence on its mysteriousness, fibromyalgia is often misunderstood as nothing more than a one-size-fits-all diagnosis invented to pacify female patients with no visible symptoms—and indeed, it is sometimes misused this way. Even musician Kathleen Hanna, who was ultimately diagnosed with Lyme disease and who actively promotes awareness of invisible illness, has described fibromyalgia in this context. In an interview with Film.com, she explains:

"I had a doctor who dumped me in the fibromyalgia category and I just got up and left. I was just like, fuck you, I don't have fibromyalgia. That's just, to me, from what I've learned, it's a medical diagnosis dumping ground for women. They just *dump* you in there when they don't know what you have."

△△△△△△△△△△△△△△△△△

The answer to the Sphinx's riddle, by the way, is a person: Four legs when they crawl as a baby, two legs when they walk, and three in old age when they use a cane.

Though I currently walk on two legs, I have a friend who was also diagnosed with fibromyalgia who uses a wheelchair. I'm not sure how many legs the Sphinx would count that as.

The tremendous difference between my friend's symptoms and mine makes me think of Hanna's suspicion of the fibromyalgia diagnosis. While I do believe it's useful—at least in the limited sense that there is value in giving a name to something with no name and thereby giving it legitimacy—it's only a starting point. The diagnosis only names the mystery. It doesn't begin to solve it.

The Protective Mundane
JAYINEE BASU

My biological interior is freaking out. My shell is expanding and shrinking in localized and minute ways. I feel encephalitic. I skip class for the second time this week and cry.

(To be honest, this whole thing is mostly my blanket's fault. I have felt imprisoned by this blanket in what seems like a Chinese finger trap kind of torture, where every struggle to escape makes its creepy microfibers close in on me even more. Inventing a blanket that prevents its inhabitant from venturing out to seek food, water or sex seems like a dumb evolutionary move. I am making a mental note to write a strongly worded letter to its manufacturers, who will no doubt see this as some sort of mock-angry praise.)

Anyway, so I'm here, stuck in this blanket, thinking about all the ways in which growing up is hard and unpleasant, when I begin to cry even harder realizing that it's not hard, actually, it's exceedingly easy. Life is very, very easy for me because I have all these resources at hand that I'm wasting, essentially. I get very angry at myself and start counting the ways in which I'm failing other human beings. Performing whiteness is a prerequisite to being able to do anything with any degree of institutional support. I realize I have gotten pretty good at this performance. Now nothing I do to reclaim or reexamine Indian anything will ring true, because I've already vetted myself with whiteness and am therefore safe. Safety in this case feels cowardly and like a betrayal to those who can't cast their skin off so easily.

In an effort to escape the blanket, I take two caffeine pills and look up "suicide methods" on the Internet. I find a site that supplies a matrix of considerations based on time, pain level and efficacy. I'm not going to go into it because I already feel weird saying that this resource exists, but basically I start eyeing my room for structures that can support a weight of ~100 pounds. My room is a very tall and very small square with no protrusions of any kind except a doorknob that regularly falls out.

I am getting really restless. I look at all the clothes hanging on my garment rack. A wool peacoat derives visual strength by invoking a naval power that brought India to its knees. An epaulet on a military jacket confers hierarchical status. Knockoff Swedish Hasbeens in wood and blue leather speak to Nordic genteelness. My hair is artificially lighter than black. I love minimalism and Dutch-inspired fonts. I've only dated white men. The website says to wait a week before taking any kind of action. I agree that this is reasonable. But I like being prepared. I write a really stupid draft of a suicide note that is not worth describing. I step outside to a beautiful summer evening. I wear the wool coat.

The walk to the hardware store feels nice. I need rope and zip ties. (If an alibi becomes necessary, I will say that I am going crabbing and need these zip ties to affix chicken wings to a net.) I feel good because I feel determined. As I walk, I try to feel hatred, or at least anger, toward white people. It is impossible. Some type of looped cognitive circuit ends up rerouting all anger back to me, which is redundant at this point. I don't want to be an adult who becomes so good at not freaking out that she begins to consider freaking out a bad thing. My memories of being teased for not being able to speak English are flattened. Anything that I can call upon to direct rage outward feels thin. My body can bury its trauma peculiarly well and this scares me. A person without the memories of their formation is not a person.

. . .

The hardware store is closed. I am extremely annoyed by this. I Yelp more hardware stores in the area. They are all closed. It is only 6:00 p.m. on a weeknight in a major metropolitan city. What the hell.

I walk over to a taqueria and eat a shrimp burrito. I feel kind of dizzy and consider what just happened. I don't feel guilty for performing whiteness. It's a survival technique. But I do feel guilty for being successful at it. It seems to indicate a treacherous ability to morph.

Later that night, I climb a radio tower to look at the eclipse with my boyfriend and his roommate. The Blood Moon keeps slipping behind shawls of cloud. We yell at it every time. I was hoping for a bloodier moon, one that might nod at what a weird day it's been. We make predictions about whether we'll be able to see the eclipse at its scheduled appearance, which is a little past midnight. We can't see it and go home.

All Thy Waves
ANNIE DAWID

For my soul is full of troubles: and my life draweth nigh unto the grave.
I am counted with them that go down into the pit: I am as a man that hath no strength.
Thou hast laid me in the lowest pit, in darkness, in the deeps.
Thy wrath lieth hard upon me, and thou hast afflicted me with all thy waves.

from Psalm 88

During my last sojourn in That Place, I could listen only to Marian Anderson and Paul Robeson singing mournful, soothing gospel. I could read only literature from the nineteenth century and earlier. In the solipsism of my condition, I discovered that King David's Psalms described depression with beauty and accuracy, and I found some solace there. I ate only cereal, and that with effort. I could not bear the sun and prayed for rain. Nights were marginally better, when I did not have to confront the light. In the wooded park where I walked my dogs, I found the darkest places and the least-trod paths. On one bend of a trail I'd never seen before, I discovered the hanging tree. Like a car wreck, it drew me back again and again. I didn't want to study it, to want what it promised, but I was defenseless against its allure. Every afternoon I walked around the old oak, admiring its solid, sturdy arm under which I believed I would achieve my final rest, like a bird, nesting. As school was out, I did not teach and had no daily obligations. I was six months pregnant—six months off my meds.

Six months earlier, the proverbial biological clock inside my body suddenly wound and humming, I thanked all the powers, gods and spirits as I read the results of my blood test. A hitherto unknown sensation of peace flooded through my veins as I walked alone across the OB/GYN waiting room. With my gray hair, I appeared twenty years older than all the other women who sat, expectantly awaiting news, alongside husbands, boyfriends, sisters and mothers.

Despite a decade of therapy and medication, depression would inevitably follow elation, but my brand-new condition seemed somehow outside the parameters of that lifelong template. Proverbially, I glowed. Never once experiencing morning sickness, I gloated, considering myself of stronger stuff than a friend who puked every morning for the first three months. Wanting a healthy, natural child, I stopped taking anything that might harm Helen/Isaiah—I chose to be surprised by my child's sex—including alcohol, tobacco, refined sugar and antidepressants.

Only many months later did I recall a psychopharmacologist, whom I'd once consulted when it seemed my ordinary medications and excellent therapist were no longer able to keep me outside That Place. After testing me, the doctor decided I'd been misdiagnosed and said my real problem was Obsessive-Compulsive Disorder, which often masquerades as depression. Obsessive thoughts and behaviors described me perfectly; Dr. H. had healed me with a new description, or so I wanted to believe. He prescribed Luvox, and for a while all was rosy, with my spanking new label and a medication that sounded like love. Should I ever become pregnant, he insisted, I would need to return and be prescribed an antidepressant appropriate for pregnancy. Perhaps I filed that information in the back of my brain. Or maybe, even then, I thought I knew better; pregnancy itself, I presumed, would be the medicine for what ailed me.

Initially, it was. Pregnant, I felt gleeful and generous. Knowing my reputation, my students were perhaps surprised to confront this roly-poly, silver-haired earth mother, quite the opposite of the normally tough, take-no-nonsense professor of college lore. As I didn't disclose my pregnancy until safely past the common miscarriage timeline, students and colleagues alike must have assumed that this change in my spirit came with approaching forty.

"Lighten up" was advice I'd heard all my life and always found banal, inappropriate in a world smeared in suffering. But during that first trimester, for the first time, it made sense: the world seemed full of light. Until April 20, 1999, when Columbine shut me down.

• • •

That summer of 1999, abruptly battened inside That Place, I blamed the massacre for such rude transport, its fusillade of child-inspired violence restoring the veil, obscuring the light I had come to trust, foolishly, as my new abode. Columbine murdered my fragile optimism. The Colorado high school, which I'd driven past many times, was a few minutes from an old friend's home; her daughters would attend that school someday. Columbine's particular horror reemphasized—because I had indeed forgotten—the true nature of existence. What had I been thinking to bring a child into a world of Columbines? For the first time, added to familiar depression, I felt constant anxiety. Hoping for a simple solution, I eliminated all caffeine, took baths and drank calming tea. But with prodigious time to fill, no longer able to concentrate on the small print of *David Copperfield* or *New Grub Street*, I worried.

I worried about everything I had not worried about before: I couldn't afford a child, I thought. I couldn't provide the support Helen/Isaiah would need from a single parent. Most importantly and obviously, I didn't have the mental stamina to be a parent, just as I had always believed to be true about myself until the biological clock startled me with its alarm at thirty-six, muffling previous fears and good sense.

In the most painful part of that turning from joy to sorrow, a close friend made it known she thought I would fail to be a good mother, due to my proclivity toward depression, from which she also suffered. Before the turning, I scoffed at her words, hurt but in no way destroyed. I read her many-paged, handwritten letter on yellow legal paper as I walked jauntily up a path in Forest Park, in the days when I felt powerful and free, walking my two mutts with my big belly and no worries. I threw the letter away; what was the purpose of it? Did she believe her words would prompt me toward a late-term abortion because she thought I was incapable of mothering? I laughed at how wrong she was, how limited in her imagination. After the turning, I could only agree: she knew me better than I knew myself, I thought. She knew the true me, the me who was at core a depressed and hopeless self, certainly not mother material.

· · ·

When I was twelve, my mother tried to kill herself. After that middle-of-the-night, dreamlike event darkened my life with despair, I distorted ordinary problems with the possibility of a suicidal solution. Only in my early twenties, with a good therapist, did I begin to understand this distortion of my adolescence, the way I had shouldered my mother's depression in the hope of saving her. But understanding did not enlighten me. To the contrary, I found such new awareness more frightening than my pre-analysis ignorance, so I drank to keep it at bay.

A female friend and I visited bars together and drank until we could hardly see, often winding up in strangers' beds. We practiced what now seems like obviously suicidal behavior—and which probably appeared that way to anyone less inebriated at the time.

At thirty-nine, however, I believed myself beyond such delusional thinking and self-destructive acts. Hadn't I spent many years and thousands of dollars on the psychiatrist's couch? Hadn't I pushed beyond my fear of medication's disrepute and tried most every pharmaceutical manufactured to facilitate recovery? Wasn't I completely in charge of a life that appeared to outsiders accomplished and full? And finally, wasn't I fantastically lucky to get pregnant so easily at such a late date when many women of my age were struggling to do so? No longer the caricature of an unhappy post-adolescent roaming the San Francisco hills at night, an A-student binge drinking on weekends and sleeping with men whose names I didn't want to remember. I was a professor, published and sober. Not only did I see myself as too sophisticated for a black-and-white worldview, but I felt it unworthy and selfish of a woman in the upper-middle-class tax bracket to imagine she was suffering. So much of the world lived in misery; I had no right to my despair.

· · ·

The most helpful thing a doctor ever told me was the following: on scans of severely depressed people, whole sections of their brains remain unilluminated, completely out of service.

In the dusk of my suicidal depression and the seventh month of my pregnancy, after trying to hang myself with the red dog leash—too short—on a rafter in the basement—too flimsy for my bulk—I ended up on the psychiatrist's couch. My OB/GYN nurse practitioner had sent me there after requiring weekly visits to her office, simply to make me appear for appointments, and witnessing, at the start of my last trimester, a sudden failure to thrive. Instead of gaining, I lost weight, and, despite the apparent health of my fetus, I was inquiring about how to "adopt out" the child who would shortly be born to me. After the inadequate rafter experience, and an afternoon with a shard of glass in the bathtub, I concluded that I needed to kill myself *after* the birth. For an adult of sound mind—which I believed myself to possess—to commit suicide was a right in a world in which one had control of one's destiny—a privilege on a planet where most had no such agency. But to murder another was unconscionable.

So I decided to live—for a while, at any rate, until my due date of September 1—and to see the doctor who, according to my nurse practitioner, had lots of experience with depressed pregnant women. Having only heard of *post*partum depression, I considered myself an anomaly, depressed at the wrong time, an asshole to be wanting to die while a friend my age in another city had been trying for years to conceive and failing.

. . .

Why did the doctor's description of a depressed brain's malfunction perforate my darkness? Despite all my reading, education, and therapy, there remained inside me enough of my German father's stoicism to deplore my condition as symptomatic of weakness, an indicator of a feeble will. After all, my father had escaped the Nazis and hadn't succumbed to depression. He'd lost his mother at twelve, most of his family had been exterminated in his twenties, his first grandchild had died of an obscure, genetic Jewish disease, and he'd had to commit his wife and son to psychiatric wards more than once, but he'd never been depressed, or so he claimed. What was my failing, if not weakness? As the smart daughter, the accomplished child most like my father, I could not admit likeness to my pathetic, crazy, death-desiring mother.

Whole sections of my brain, said Doctor O, were either operating at sub-par levels or not functioning at all. Like the outer world, the inside of my brain had slowed itself to crawl in darkness. Studies had proved that the eyes of severely depressed people could not recognize all the colors in the spectrum, he told me. It was as if the patient had suffered a head injury in a motorcycle accident, or fallen from a height onto concrete. This scientific fact, something empirical that even my steely, brilliant father could not deny, managed to penetrate my despair. To my mind, the doctor's likening of a mental state to a physical one reduced the stigma, making my condition seem less a question of will than of brain chemistry. Certain medications, Doctor O insisted, could help me while not harming Helen/Isaiah. Because my due date was so close, and I knew babies could be born at seven or eight months without long-term, life-damaging results, I decided to accept his counsel. If I could live long enough to deliver the baby safely, to hand him or her over to a loving stranger, then it would be enough. I started on a low dose of Paxil, which he hoped would diminish my anxiety as well.

. . .

Each day of the new med regime and regular appointments with Doctor O, I struggled to feel a millimeter better, to detect an iota of improvement inside me. Did the light hurt a bit less today? Did I feel a trifle less unhinged as I managed to eat a meal out with Steve and Baba, my close, quasi-parental friends? At the diner I managed a milkshake, and afterward, window-shopping on the way to Ben & Jerry's for Baba's lemon sherbet, I ducked into an upscale hardware store's entryway and began to cry. Steve had been telling a story and stopped, mid-sidewalk, to find me gone. In the alcove, when I told them I wanted to give my baby away, they didn't raise their voices in shock, or tell me I was absurd. "You're feeling that bad, huh," Steve said, rubbing my back as I wiped my eyes, leaning incongruously against the display of fancy gardening tools speckled with packages of heirloom tomato seeds.

"Oh honey," said Baba, hugging me. "It's not going to be like this always."

. . .

One Friday, Baba and I went shopping for a bassinet, the last big purchase I had yet to make. (Evidently, I didn't foresee giving up the baby until after I had made use of the perfect bassinet.) It was hot, my car had no air-conditioning, and we stopped for something cold before heading to the baked flatlands where Babies"R"Us had its outlet. Sitting in the drive-through at Burgerville USA, I discovered one could get shots of espresso in a mocha milkshake. A former coffee junkie, I'd been without caffeine for months, and I still don't know what possessed me to ask for a double, but I did.

Almost immediately, I began to feel better, more like the self I remembered. In the back of a horrid warehouse-like emporium, I found The Bassinet—unpainted wicker and Victorian, with wheels to move it from room to room. The cushion and pillow were soft white cotton, trimmed with eyelets, and I could picture my baby inside it, resting peacefully. The price was more than I'd planned on spending, but I bought it anyway, encouraged by Baba to trust my instinct—a certainty I hadn't felt for months. All afternoon I chatted and even laughed. The caffeine had powered me back into life. My first birthing class was the following morning, and I was looking forward to it. That night, I never fell asleep. I stayed up reading *The Birth Partner*, feeling so alive I couldn't shut my eyes. Though I blamed the caffeine for my inability to rest, I was simultaneously grateful. That double-espresso mocha milkshake appeared to have re-set my clock, springing me back into the land of the living.

When B picked me up at 8:30 a.m. for the class, weird sensations pulsed inside me, new ones. While she drove, I looked up my symptoms in the book, and we decided I must be experiencing false labor pains. But they wouldn't go away, and by the time of our first break at eleven, I was feeling strange indeed. Are they contractions? the teacher asked me. How would I know? I'd never felt one before. As my due date was still three weeks away, they had to be something else. Then I discovered I was bleeding.

At the hospital, after we'd stopped at the house to

pick up clothes and music and books, I was chagrined to discover I would not be put under the care of a midwife, as planned; I would be under the MD on duty due to the abrasion of my placenta, which was apparently causing the bleeding. Still fueled by caffeine and wired from lack of sleep and powered by whatever else was going on inside me, I could feel another kind of turning upon me. The MD had the bedside manners of a crude plumber, and I was damned if he would deliver my baby. Our mutual antipathy gave me strength, and I determined to last out his twelve-hour shift.

The bleeding stopped, I was given a room in the midwifery labor-and-delivery wing, and it appeared I was indeed going to deliver this baby early. After eight months and one week, perhaps catalyzed by my double-espresso, Helen/Isaiah was ready to enter the world. Or perhaps s/he had sensed my turning and knew *I* was ready.

Approximately twenty-four hours after being admitted to the hospital, I gave birth to Isaiah Max, nineteen inches long, five and a half pounds, whose only apparent trouble was tachycardia, excessively rapid breathing common to early arrivals. Later I would learn this condition was not unusual for babies born to antidepressant-popping mothers.

Friends had cleaned the house and walked the dogs, making everything ready for us. The beautiful bassinet was parked in the living room beside my gliding rocking chair with its gliding ottoman, a group present from colleagues. Isaiah had taken to my nipple with gusto, and the following days passed in an easy dreaminess. Baba stayed over and Steve brought us meals, my favorite Super-Dog Supreme Burritos from across town. When I saw the red dog leash, I didn't think of the oak in the woods, waiting for me. Instead, I hooked it to Ralph's or

Pete's collar, strapped Isaiah in my Snuggly, and strolled the park with my baby and dogs. I walked in the meadows, avoiding the trees. I put the psalms away.

. . .

But heard, half-heard, in the stillness
Between two waves of the sea.
Quick now, here, now, always—
A condition of complete simplicity
(Costing not less than everything)

from "Little Gidding"

The Woman and the Hippopotamus
DANA FASCIANO

None of us wanted to be in the hospital that first night when they wheeled you into the cafeteria during dinner. We couldn't eat as we watched your jaws struggle to remember the mechanics of chewing. The skin on your skull was so thin that every vein showed in a web of purple. Your blonde hair hung like ragweed around your sunken eyes.

I wanted to know what you had looked like when you were a woman. Before you had lost hips, breasts, and your blood. I wanted to hear you speak without the drunken slur of malnutrition.

The next day you were on bed rest because you had starved away all of the muscles around your heart.

We were the same age. The doctors didn't want you to be alone. I moved into your room that afternoon. "Look at me," you said. "I'm a hippopotamus." I offered a consoling smile, touched my diminishing breasts. I knew that it was impossible to be both a woman and a hippopotamus.

My #RealResume
ANDREA FREUND

When I started my blog, I imagined the day that I'd be writing this post: a heart-warming retrospective about how I *used to be*. I couldn't wait to share all the wonderful life lessons I'd gained from a horribly trying—and now over—experience.

Well, today is most definitely <u>not</u> that day. I've been privately battling this thing for five years, and I'm tired of waiting, of making progress but not *enough* progress. The secrecy and loneliness is exhausting.

So here's the truth: I have an eating disorder.
Have. As in presently.

Sharing this part of me goes against my every instinct. Over the years, I've gotten pretty good at hiding my struggles. I've learned to put on a polished, perfect front—to be charming and witty (but never unfeminine or aggressive), to get the right degree and the right job, to never repeat the same mistake twice (or preferably, never make a mistake at all), to stay slim, to stay small. Yet my eating disorder is a constant and vivid reminder of my own imperfection and my failure to be all of those things. Speaking about it makes me feel excruciatingly exposed, like pale skin under a blinding, burning sun.

So why am I writing about it? Why put myself through these feelings of intense vulnerability? I often tell myself that my eating disorder is none of the world's business (it's not like I go around sharing my blood pressure or family medical history). But I know that's not the reason I've kept silent. No, the truth is that I've been trying to protect myself—or more accurately, to protect my eating disorder. Speaking about it means I can't pretend I am "just fine" any longer. It means committing to change.

I wasn't always sick, of course. I was twenty-one before my eating disorder became "official" by clinical standards. But looking back, I can see that my beliefs about myself were distorted long before the restricting, bingeing, and throwing up began. I was still a child when I started believing that I wasn't "ok" just as I was. Yet it's hard to pinpoint exactly when those thoughts first occurred, and it's even harder to say why. By age twenty-one, that sentiment (and the constant self-beration that came with it) was such an ingrained part of my identity that I found it impossible to trace it back to an external source. It was simply who I was: not good enough.

After much therapy, I can at least identify some of the things that contributed to that belief. For example, as the only girl and baby of my family, I constantly felt like I was holding others back, like I was two or three years behind in life. Instead of realizing that it was normal to not to be as fast or smart or mature as my older siblings, I blamed myself for failing to keep up. This feeling was exacerbated by the constant "harmless" teasing I endured from relatives for being too sensitive, too young, too much of a girl. I became afraid to assert my needs out of fear that doing so would be further evidence that I was "difficult" and "the baby."

At school, I didn't quite fit in either. I had friends,

but I was never the first one they picked to invite to things. I often felt like I was an afterthought, the person you call when you need a warm body to fill the space or, in the case of middle school, because your mother told you to.

Eventually I grew up, but I discovered that as a woman, my body was just another thing to make me feel like I wasn't good enough, another thing for others to critique and comment on. From strangers on the street to big-shot women's "lifestyle" magazines, I received—and continue to receive—constant messages about how I should look. Even my own relatives would playfully tease me with comments like "a moment on the lips, forever on the hips," while my male cousins received praise for their hearty appetites because they were "growing boys."

No part of me was sacred, not as a child and not as a young adult. After so many years of worrying that a cruel joke or an uncomfortable comment was only moments away, I no longer felt safe in my own skin.

While none of these things was the singular "cause" of my eating disorder, they led me to form a dangerous conclusion: if I simply never failed, never gave the world anything to criticize, then I could finally feel safe.

By age sixteen, I had firmly latched onto this idea. I got perfect grades, limited myself to a small salad at lunch each day, pushed myself to go to the gym no matter how much my muscles ached. My obsession with perfection wasn't limited to my appearance, but my body gave me something tangible to fixate on. It was something I felt like I could—and should—control.

I believed that being perfect would make me impenetrable to the cruelty of the world—and to some degree, it did. People complimented me for being so accomplished. They told my mother what a great daughter she had raised. Over time, that perfect version of myself became my identity. Yet as other people's criticism diminished, something far worse took its place: my own inner critic, who was more vicious than any person in the outside world. I told myself that I had raised other people's expectations of me, and that if I let myself go, even a little, they would see the pathetic, disgusting person I was underneath it all.

To appease that critical voice and distract myself from the larger questions of my own self-worth, I ruthlessly stuck to my unforgiving routine of working out daily and eating less and less. But the critical voice couldn't be appeased. It berated me, shouting that I was still too fat. It told me that I lacked willpower and discipline, that I was disgusting. And so I tried harder, restricting even more and never thinking that what I was doing was unhealthy.

But bodies can only put up with so much abuse. My junior year of college, my body finally staged a mutiny. I was *hungry*, physically and emotionally. My willpower to "keep myself in check" was slipping, and I felt like I was falling apart. So one day, about halfway into fall semester, that fear and anxiety simply became too much for me, and I decided to try to throw up my meal. I knew it could be done (thanks in large part to some really questionable educational videos shown during high school health class), but that first time was hard. I could barely get any of the food back up. But the next day I tried again, and again, and like any good perfectionist, I soon mastered it.

Over the next five years, I became entrenched in my bulimia, often throwing up multiple times a day. The eating disorder promised me, at least for a moment, a blissful escape from having to try *so hard* at being perfect. After I graduated college and started living on my own in the real world, giving in to my disorder became all too easy; there was no one watching me closely, no communal dining halls, no obstacles to my disorder.

Throughout this time, I didn't tell a soul, but I was terrified someone would discover the truth. As much as I needed my eating disorder to feel "ok," I was also deeply ashamed of it. I felt it was my fault. I didn't fit the stereotype of, say, a fifteen-year-old girl, pressured by her peers and too young to recognize what was happening. I was a well-educated adult, and I hadn't endured anything that I deemed "sufficiently traumatic" to justify developing an eating disorder. I told myself I should have known better. While I could rationalize restricting my food and over-exercising, it's hard to pretend that making yourself throw up isn't dangerous and unhealthy. My critical voice told me that my disorder was indicative of a deeper, fundamental flaw in me—that I simply lacked discipline. The longer I relied on my disorder, the deeper my shame got.

On my twenty-fifth birthday, I finally hit a breaking point. There I was, alone in my room, my heart racing and my head dizzy after throwing up my latest meal. Up until this point, I'd been convinced that if I just got my act together and showed a little more discipline, I could get over this disorder by myself. But in reality, I was out of control. Hours of my day were spent throwing up. I kept spreadsheets of how many calories I'd eaten. Walking up a single flight of stairs made me lightheaded. I'd made countless resolutions that tomorrow would be different, only to fail over and over and *over again*.

On that evening of my twenty-fifth birthday, I felt utterly and completely helpless. It was an emotional low that no amount of food and no number on the scale could mask. I believed nothing could be worse than the pain I felt in that moment. I wanted out. And so I did the thing I had been so afraid of: I reached out for help.

Within a week, I had taken a leave of absence from work and checked myself into an intensive outpatient treatment facility. I completed the intake process quickly, filling out forms and scheduling admissions interviews like I was on autopilot. I feared that if I paused, even for a second, I would talk myself out of my decision to get help.

I gave myself four weeks off work to get "all better." Of course, I realize now how ridiculous that expectation was, but I wanted to cross recovery off my to-do list like it was on par with doing the laundry or buying car insurance. Just like before, I kept telling myself that if I just had discipline, I could kick this thing.

The treatment facility wasn't exactly a perfect fit either. I got into more than a few, ahem, *heated* arguments with the staff there. I resented the way they walked around with their clipboards at mealtime, checking off my different food groups. I couldn't stand the air of superiority their "normal" eating habits afforded them. I hated the way they assumed I was always trying to cheat the system (what did they think I was doing? Secretly stuffing portions into my purse or something?). I had checked myself in voluntarily, but their approach felt punitive. I wasn't viewed as "Andrea, a woman struggling with an eating disorder," but instead only as "the patient"—and a willfully resistant one at that. I didn't feel respected. I didn't feel inspired.

Perhaps worst of all was lying to my friends and family during that time. They'd ask me how work was going and I'd say something vague like "Oh same old, same old. Keeping busy." How could I tell them that my every waking moment was spent thinking about my eating disorder, thinking about food, thinking about my weight? That I hadn't been to my job in weeks and that my career was the last thing on my mind? If I'd felt like I was living a lie before, it was *nothing* compared to this.

Just to complicate things further, around that same time my parents' marriage was falling apart—and if I'm completely honest, a small dark part of me was grateful. Suddenly, there was no fooling the world that we were this perfect upper-middle-class, all-American family. Our neat little world was crumbling down around us, and for the first time, I felt a little bit of freedom—like maybe it was okay for me to say out loud that I wasn't perfect either.

But even then, I could only whisper it. I told my brother and sister-in-law the truth about my disorder (in vague, non-scary terms—the idea of *anyone* having the mental image of me bingeing or throwing up ~~was~~ is horrifying to me). But I was afraid to tell anyone else. I still thought I could hide my disorder from everyone until I was "cured" and ready to come out of the closet as a healthy, carefree woman. I thought I could have close, authentic relationships and *still* keep my struggle secret from the people I loved. I told myself these lies over and over until I believed them.

I ended up staying at the treatment facility for nearly two months. While I made minimal progress there, I will credit the program with one thing: it taught me how to start talking about my disorder. To say words like "purge" and "bulimia" and "restriction." It helped chip away at some of the shame. By enrolling in the treatment program, I'd opened the door to recovery. It meant I couldn't put my head back into the sand (no matter how much I wanted to at times) and pretend that I was fine or that I could get better on my own. It meant I couldn't ignore the part of me that wanted to be free of my disorder more than the part of me that wanted to be perfect and in control.

After I left the treatment program, I decided to try a

different approach. I hired a new therapist and started going regularly to group support meetings in San Francisco. I started making progress, but after about eight months, I hit a standstill. I was bingeing and purging a little less than before, but my inner critic was still as loud as ever. My therapist, God ~~hate~~ love her, kept pushing me to tell more people about my disorder and to start asking for support. She asserted that if I wanted proof that it was safe to be myself again, then I had to let people see the real me, and that included my struggle with my eating disorder. I told her NO. NO, *no, no. No.* I got angry at her nagging. But if there is one thing I've come to realize through this process, it's that when I get pissed off at my therapist, it's usually because she is right (I don't think she had a public blog post in mind, but hey—when I commit, I *commit*).

Before I could share this post, there was one thing I had to do: tell my mom about my eating disorder. My mom and I have always been close, and I couldn't bear the thought of upsetting her, of making her cry. All she's ever wanted was for me to be happy and healthy. And I had failed at both of those things. How could I disappoint her like that?

It took every ounce of my courage to pick up that phone and dial my mom, hundreds of miles away in Texas. Our family had just gone through one major upheaval with my parents' split, and I was about to add another. I'd practiced what I was going to say, but the words felt like a heavy lump in my throat and there was a lot of nervous sweating happening by the time she answered the call with her cheerful, "Hi Sweetie."

"Mom, I have something to tell you."

As soon as the words came out of my mouth, all the tears I'd been holding back, all the pain and inadequacy I'd been carrying around with me for years came pouring out. Despite my fear, I was finally speaking my truth. I wasn't alone in this anymore. And guess what? My mom had already known something was wrong (moms are clever like that); she was just waiting for me to tell her.

And now I'm telling all of you. I cannot pretend to be perfect any longer. I cannot hide this constant presence in my life. I was desperate to be viewed as beautiful, intelligent, talented, and successful—and *only* as those things. I was afraid that having an eating disorder would make those other qualities untrue.

But as I've worked on my recovery, I've also realized that even the most talented and successful people among us are not invincible. Yet many of us, myself included, try to present a perfect front to the rest of the world, because perfection feels safe. Perfection promises freedom from criticism and judgment. But when we hide our struggles, we also hide our strength. I used to think that having an eating disorder made me weak. But I'm starting to see how much strength it takes for me to just get through the day, considering that even the most mundane activities—like eating normally in front of others—are a battle. Yet I face those battles *every day*, even when the road gets bumpy (and it gets *real* bumpy). That can't be weakness.

I've learned a lot during my recovery process so far (I guess this post actually did end up including all those "wonderful life lessons" I imagined), but **I am not recovered**. Not yet. But I believe I will be someday. And while right now my life often feels like a mess, it feels good (and terrifying) to finally be honest about it.

The practical part of me worries that sharing this information so publicly will come back to bite me. I'd be lying if I said I wasn't worried about damaging the way my boss or my future employers view me when they inevitably run a Google search on me. But speaking about my eating disorder doesn't suddenly make me less capable at my job, less talented, less *me*. It doesn't negate all the other things I am. It's just another addition to my resume.

I am Andrea Freund. I graduated from Stanford with a BS in Biology. I work in corporate communications. I am a writer, a dreamer, and sarcastic to a fault. And yes, I have bulimia. That's my #RealResume. And it's still pretty kick-ass.

A Transsexual's Manifesto

GINA MARIE BERNARD

So you want to know about the duality
of my identity—my transsexuality?
It's true, I may seem a bit of a rarity.
Spent many years in therapy.
All because I hated my plurality.
Questioned my sanity.
Each breath I took reminded me
of the supreme irony of my entirety.
Some claim my immortality is in jeopardy.
That I make a mockery of morality;
that I will spend an eternity
burning for the enormity
of my non-conformity.
But am I a monstrosity?
Is the woman you see inherently
some biological anomaly?

How horribly we react to dissimilarity.

So, please, temporarily
set aside any need to categorically
assign me to familiarity.
I'm here primarily—and with all sincerity—

to assert without temerity
that WE—you and me—ALL fall
on a continuum of diversity.
Don't agree? Well, allow me an analogy.

Like any book, I have a cover,
but open me up and you'll discover
that my narrative is not some "other";
rather, it is just "another."
I hope my critique—
these words that I speak—
will pique your curiosity.
Tweak you consciously
to the distinct possibility
that our stories, though unique, also speak
to the similarity of the human condition;
to a shared homogeny.
And it's my position—my mission—
to get you to listen.
We're all the same!
And my aim shall remain:
To claim that it is insane,
this need to proclaim
that it's "us" vs. "them."
How banal! How inane!
Why must you stare?
Or worse, glare
with hate in your eyes? Or dare
to pass judgment—
to mock and to jeer—
to blare ignorant obscenities
like *faggot* or *queer*?
So you sneer
at the way I appear?
Who the fuck cares?

I don't recall asking you
ever to share.
Who are you
to declare
that I'm a freak or a whore?
And spare me your
sanctimonious prayers!
I'm aware
that I inspire
in you an unfathomable fear;
that you find me bizarre
and dangerously impure;
but you can keep your appeals—
the true way that you feel—
to yourself, if you please.
Grow up! I'm not going anywhere.
I'm the girl next door,
And none of your slurs
will adhere to me
or force me to be
what you find acceptable, see?
I refuse to be defined by
your childish insecurities,
or your profound inadequacies.
The prejudice belying
your "love the sinner" insincerities—
what a bunch of hypocritical piety!

Yes, it's a dangerous world for Ts like me
who tease apart the threads of an
artificial gender binary.
Who refuse to be abused
or to appease
others' unease.
So I'm a threat—a disease.

And for many years,
I accepted these labels;
expected the tables
never to turn,
and inside it burned
that I was unable
to remain stable,
or to foresee
the cost of ignoring my reality.
I was a dysphoric amputee.
Cut off—degree by degree—
from any degree of certainty.
God, the humanity!

As a kid, what I did
to keep my secret hidden
was I buried my Id—
screwed down the lid.
Deposited HER so far beneath the grid
that SHE was forbid
to do any good.
And so my personality slid
away; stayed away,
and amid all the gray
I prayed each day
for HER to simply go away.
But HER ember burned
and SHE yearned
to be heard.
Refused to be ignored.
My reality blurred.
And though interred,
in her sepulcher SHE stirred.
The result? My life became
a theater of the absurd.

A married man; a father of two,
hiding a secret nobody knew.
Until I told my wife—
the love of my life;
my revelation struck like a knife
and hit her out of the blue.
I didn't come out of the closet;
instead, I dragged her in.
Begged her not to leave,
to be complicit—to practice collusion.
To help me deceive
through exclusion and seclusion.
But this was a burden,
and resulted in confusion.
She came to the conclusion
our marriage was just an illusion.

The problem with living a lie—a version
of who it is you are submerging—
is that it creates personality subversion,
and the requisite coercion
creates a climate of aversion.
Aversion begets perversion
of who you are as a person.
The result is that you become a psychological
    orphan,
a Martian—alien life form
swallowing truth and projecting deceit
through painful contortion.
You're displaced, erased:
identity abortion.

My condition worsened;
I became someone I hated.
Existentialist angst

exacerbated by this cosmic joke
to which I'd been fated.
I silently waited. My life stopped—
I was in a state of stasis:
Alone, no help in sight, no oasis.
Deflated, plagued by mental masturbation,
I berated myself; vacated myself; negated myself.
Sated myself with a secret self
that destroyed mental health:
Online trysts that consisted
of lustful predators
all too willing to assist
in validating my existence.
In violating my innocence.
But I knew it was wrong,
that I had to desist.
Yet, I couldn't.
In the midst of this mess
that I was powerless to resist,
I clenched my fists;
I gritted my teeth, I was so pissed.
My life, one big ball of shit—
a cancerous cyst.
Jesus Christ, I wanted
to slit open my wrists!
I went numb and succumbed
to their licentious thrusts.
I was groped; I was kissed.
And like any woman with no self-esteem,
I was summarily dismissed.

Divorce imminent,
facing abandonment,
feeling my existence
was one abhorrent experiment.

I was emotionally spent
and the hole that had rent
my soul in two
convinced me I was through.
It was time to do
what I knew fate had led me to:
To take my life;
to put an end
to my pain and my strife;
to still the voices
that plagued me day and night;
to go toward the light;
to unplug; to drift;
to succumb to the white noise.
I gave up, made the choice.
Shotgun in hand,
I no longer gave a damn.
Percocet my backup plan,
in case cowardice
prevented me from
taking aim.

But photos of my daughters,
memories of their laughter—
the thought of leaving them
to clean up after my disaster—
made my illness seem
malicious, sinister.
My decision would freeze
their growth like winter.
Infect their tongues with blisters.
Drown their voices in a crimson
canyon of abandonment.
My death would become their burden,
innocent children left behind

to harden beneath the rumors and whispers.

So I got up. I got help. I moved on.
Truth does come with a price,
and many from my former life
have withdrawn:
disowned by my father,
his love—conditional—is now gone.
Friendships, too, have flown,
but I press on; each day begins with a new dawn.
And I am NOT alone!
I'm a roller derby queen
and Wonder Woman rolled all into one,
my daughters' love a healing balm.
I'm more than a feminine father,
but not quite their mom.
I've been reborn and I've reclaimed
the years of shame and now take ownership of this
    name.
It flows through my veins and
demands I take a stand. So, with pen in hand,
I rebrand. Do you understand?

My lament is through; instead, I give to you
a declaration—this proclamation.
A dedication to the prefix TRANS:

I transmogrify gender!
I transform minds!
Transfixed by this splendor,
I transfuse mankind!
This poem is my transcript:
A transsexual manifesto;
my translucent primal scream.
It is my transmission; it is my dream.

I am a transfigure of multiplicity.
I transpose body parts.
I'm a trans-parent, oh so witty,
a pretty father—a trans-sister—
a transitional paradox.
I hope you've been transported
by this message that I spit.
My perceptions, my transcription
supported by my transgendered heart and wit.

I leave you with this challenge:
Embrace change!
Dare to seek out the strange!
Rearrange your perspective
to accept the biggest irony—
that our individuality,
the differences we insist on seeing,
are in actuality what make us human beings.
It's a vibrant connectivity.
And I will say one last time, breathlessly,
my opus, while ostensibly about me,
is essentially a shout-out to our *shared* humanity!

Lab Limbo

JANIS BUTLER HOLM

There she was, sitting, waiting,
sitting and waiting, hoping,
sitting and waiting and hoping,
hoping the news would be good.

Sitting and waiting and hoping,
she wondered and pondered.
She wondered and pondered
and waited and hoped.
Sitting, she waited and
wondered and pondered.
She hoped for good news.
How she hoped.

Hoping, she sat and waited.
She wondered, she pondered,
she hoped, and she hoped.
She sat there, hoping,
hoping and waiting.
She wondered and pondered
and hoped.
How she hoped.

Sitting and waiting,
she hoped and wondered.
She pondered with hope
and wonder while
sitting, while waiting.
Waiting and wondering,
sitting and pondering,
she hoped for good news.
There she was.

Meditation on Mortality
JOAN ANNSFIRE

Now, for the first time, I feel a common bond with other members of the human race. I am no longer just one odd, lesbian outcast with zero interest in what I've observed to be the mainstays of American culture: child-rearing and team sports. Instead, I am experiencing something universal, something shared: the simple fact that we are all born into these fragile bodies and have but a limited amount of time on Earth.

Driving home, the blues station on my radio broadcasts a jazzy version of the song "This Little Light of Mine," and I am aware of something I've never understood before: that this is not a song about a person holding up a lantern or a candle. It's not about God either, at least not in the sense of some all-powerful dude watching over his flock. It is a song about a transcendent energy, an inner power, the light that emanates from each one of us.

My perception continues to shift in the small space of the coming weeks. I begin to devour books by, about and for people with cancer. At forty years old, even though I've watched so many of my gay male peers die of AIDS, I have never truly believed that the concept of mortality applies to me.

A dream keeps haunting me on those rare nights when I actually sleep. I am walking alone through a bombed, burned-out wasteland that looks like the aftermath of a nuclear war. As the last living creature on Earth, I roam the debris-covered streets, calling out the names of people I used to know and love. I recite the liturgy of the dead, of my mentors, of all those who have gone before.

I try to visualize nothingness. I imagine a world of infinite space and transcendent energy. I contemplate freedom from struggle. I envision rest. I imagine total oblivion.

People begin to look different to me. It's as though I am seeing them in three dimensions for the first time. I find myself weaving their stories, their unique histories, the singular circumstances of their lives. The weirdest aspect of this insight is that I seem to look changed to them as well. Strangers start conversations with me wherever I go. I sense I am giving off a new type of energy, one in which I am more deeply aware, more attuned to the community around me, to the present moment.

Tomorrow is the day of my surgery. Today, I am simply sitting at work, ridding my mind of unnecessary worries, the myriad of minute details that have kept me from truly experiencing the world. Looking out the window, I see a bruised sky hovering over rain-drenched streets. I know now that this imperfect life, in all its transient and aching splendor, is so much more than dark, wet streets full of people rushing around, as if they had someplace really important to go.

Fear, that primal scream inside my head that followed my diagnosis, has been replaced by a profound silence. If I make it through this, I vow to do all those things I had planned but never found the money or the time. I will travel, I'll write, I'll shine my little light. And, even though my surgery is still ahead, I have this unshakable sense that the worst is over.

I stand poised, on the brink of a magnificent canyon, with the universe spread out like a shining promise before me. The only thing left to do is close my eyes and leap into pure air. If my parachute opens, I will be unstoppable.

Camis

ERICA STERNIN

Before the surgery, I was given information
To help me prepare for discharge.
I was to bring a camisole with pouches for the
    drains—
Covered by insurance.

Drains? I thought. *What,*
Are we installing a plumbing system?
Sure enough, before I'm feeling brave,
The nurse opens my gown and
There's a sewer system
Where my breast used to be.

On the website, I notice mammaried models
Demonstrating the use of the "mastectomy cami."
The one with pockets for pus bottles,
Drains
"Easily removable for emptying."
The one with "pockets for breast forms."
So many pockets now.

The sky lightens gradually—it's all different today.
Like a nausea rising inexorably,
The "new normal" dawns.

In the Pink

JENNIFER MACBAIN-STEPHENS

I am mad at my cancer.
I use humor to deal with my cancer.
I have come to terms with my cancer.
My cancer is not mine.
I won't call my cancer my cancer.
I make video diaries.
I joined an online chat room.
I am a survivor of ten years.
I am a survivor of six years.
I am a survivor of two years.
I am at war with cancer.
I am at war with my body.
My body has turned against me.
I am winning the battle against my body.
I am losing my battle.
I beat cancer.
I love myself, but hate my cancer.
My soul does not have cancer.
The love I carry does not have cancer.
I tattooed my bald head.
I bought a $200 wig.
I shaved my head when I first found out.
I am in charge.

I am out of control.

I control the things I can control.

I let go of most things.

I forgave myself.

I forgave my husband.

I forgave my mother.

I am still here.

Some of the above statements were found on and taken from the following online breast cancer sources: Survivor Stories, The Pink Ribbon Shop, and Care of Cancer Survivors.

LEONORE HILDEBRANDT

My Seaweed Chest

The technician works discreetly, naming
neither breasts nor purpose, changing slides,
arranging parts. I hold my breath.

No mention of mammalian pleasures,
our slow, abundant gifts. In patterns
and pigments, we'll find the undeniable—

what else? Afterward, exit signs omit
a hundred subtle messages, and the asphalt,
oddly, smells of forest, of rabbit, of air.

. . .

The Examination

The skin knows the beginnings and endings.
It harbors the porous, translucent self.
It bears our recklessness.

My own skin is quickly told
—cumulatively—when I surrender
its blemishes to your sheltering hands.

. . .

Leaning Toward Recovery

Interiors. Along rooms of increasing severity,
the body's privacies are laid open,
its histories and vital signs.
Resting now under warm blankets—

my precious mortality—covered,
uncovered, stung and stitched, pulled
inside and out, handled with care,
(can I see?) my cells' microscopic secrets.

Later, walking toward the parking deck's
upper level clouds, the evening's curvature,
dulled but to resume normal activities, I can see
five smooth wildcats right where I live, at play.

Flirting With Death
KIMBERLY CONDON

Frances was not my friend. In nursing school I learned that a therapeutic relationship with a patient involved a one-sided connection. The patient's story mattered; mine did not. My job was to listen, counsel, and support, and while fondness for my patients was inevitable, a certain clinical distance was encouraged. But Fran had a lasting effect on me that I could hardly account for by calling her my patient. She wasn't my friend, but I loved her.

In 2008, Denver's Christmas Eve was cold, crystalline, and blinding in the sunlight. Many of my coworkers had children, and I had never minded working holidays. As a hospice admissions nurse, my job was to meet the patient and family, initiate immediate comfort care, and get all of the paperwork signed, in preparation for the regular nurse case manager who would make weekly visits. In a pattern typical in medicine, crises abounded in this joyful time of year. Just as I finished the last notes of the day my boss stopped me and asked if I could see one more patient. She needed a visit and lived not far from me.

Hers was one of the larger houses in a rural Colorado community. When I knocked on the door a weary young woman, baby at her hip, answered. "I'm Leslie. This is Scooter."

I stepped in and looked around the beautiful, meticulously decorated foyer. I followed them into the living room, where a man stood facing a window.

"Dad," Leslie said. "The hospice nurse is here." The man was tall and his broad shoulders tensed under a perfectly pressed yellow shirt. He didn't turn around.

Leslie explained that her mother, once a strong and successful businesswoman, was now too miserable to leave her bed. Her doctors had suggested they talk to hospice.

"Hi Mr. Mooney. I'm Kim."

The man turned to face me, extending his hand as if greeting a business associate. "Daniel Mooney."

I explained that the purpose of hospice is to support the patient and family in yielding to nature. Our goal is to help a patient to die peacefully, painlessly, and with dignity. We have nothing to do with the timeline and, contrary to some theories, we are not there to squash hope. Instead we represent a philosophical shift, from standing up to death and seeing it as the enemy to standing next to it, hand in hand, and welcoming the peace that comes from surrendering to the inevitable.

Daniel turned without speaking and walked into the bedroom.

Frances lay in bed, her skin as colorless as clay against her smudged, plum-flesh lipstick. The smell of stale sheets and bile stung my nostrils as I moved toward the bed and waited for her to open her eyes. A feeding tube in her nose supplied milky pink fluid to her cachectic frame, even as she heaved in nausea. With a pause from retching, her cracked lips pulled into a tiny smile, further stretching the delicate skin of her face. She was forty-nine years old.

"Hi Frances. I'm Kim, the hospice nurse." I leaned in close, lowering myself to her eye level. I didn't let go of her hand until she let go. When she did, I pulled a chair close to the bed.

"Were you able to sleep last night?" The room was dark but I thought she looked a little tan, perhaps from excessive bilirubin. I wondered about her liver function.

She shook her head.

"Were you in pain? Or was it the nausea that kept you up?"

"Yes," she said, smiling.

"As I ask you questions, I'm going to check you over, okay? It won't hurt, I'll be gentle." Daniel paced behind me.

I proceeded to examine her, body part by body part, without uncovering her. This took less than five minutes. She told me she hadn't eaten in a week and that she couldn't stop retching. That she was too miserable to sleep or talk. When I got down to her legs, careful not to expose both at the same time and make her feel vulnerable, Daniel stopped pacing and came up to the bedside.

His frenetic energy felt out of place in the room. "She did all that chemo. Rounds and rounds of it. Now Lea wants her to talk to hospice."

Dr. Lea Stone had a wonderful reputation as an aggressive and caring oncologist. But it seemed that she hadn't discussed the current prognosis with Frances or her family. I imagined the common euphemisms: "There's nothing more we can do." Or, "Go home and be with your family until the end." Simple, direct statements like "You are dying" are rare in medicine outside of hospice.

"Frances," I said. "Are you getting pretty tired of this?"

Finally, she spoke. "Yes." She looked at me, and then immediately looked at her husband.

"Would it be okay if I spoke to Frances alone?" I asked. Clearly, she wasn't comfortable talking about this in front of him.

Daniel's lips blanched but he didn't move.

"Daniel." Frances's voice was sharp, but she smiled. She reached her hand out to him and he kissed it. Daniel grimaced, wrinkling the skin between his eyes. Without speaking, he left the room.

I sat down in the chair next to her, leaning in.

"Let's talk about goals, okay?" She looked confused for a moment. "Your goals have changed, right? Before you were sick? After you were diagnosed?"

"Of course," she said.

"And I understand that your cancer went into remission a few months ago. I'm sure your goals were different when it came back, right?"

Her eyes welled with tears.

"You always have goals, Frances. But they have to be fluid, depending on what's happening at each moment."

She turned her head towards me, squinting a little.

I put my hand in hers and she squeezed. "The goal of hospice is to help you have a calm, peaceful, dignified death." I sat quietly as she cried.

Finally, she said, "That's the first time anyone has said that word to me. Death."

We discussed changing her medications and stopping her tube feeds. I explained that people who have begun the dying process often feel no hunger and if they try to eat, the body responds with nausea and vomiting.

"But if I don't eat," she started, taking a few gulping breaths. "Won't that mean…?"

"Frances, you can't eat now. If you stop trying, you may stop retching. You may be more comfortable." She nodded and I helped her to a sitting position. I clamped the tube, had her take a breath, and slipped it out of her nose. She wiped her face and laid back down.

Patients often tire quickly and I have to remind myself to be sensitive to their energy levels. I began to gather my things.

"I thought you were going to ask me personal questions, like if I believe in Santa Claus." She giggled and I started to see the person she must have been before her illness.

"Well, I was going to ask you about your shirt," I said. She wore a man-sized white t-shirt with "I (heart) Lesbians" across the front.

"It's a joke. My husband's shirt," she said.

Though I don't usually share personal information with patients, for some reason I said, "Well, I love them too."

"Oh!" she squealed, her face turning red. "I didn't mean to offend."

"I'm not offended at all." We both laughed out loud.

Not every patient appreciates integrating humor into a conversation about death, but Frances clearly shared my style. I thought about how easily we could have been friends, under different circumstances.

As I stood to leave I asked, "If there was one thing I could do to make you feel better, what would it be?"

"I want to hold my grandson."

By the end of my visit Fran and I had established a connection that reminded me of why I was drawn to this type of nursing. Many specialties require the cultivation of long-term relationships. Some nurses become attached to their patients and families—seeing them almost daily and becoming part of their lives. I gravitated toward areas, like hospice intake, that require practitioners to "get in and get out." Perhaps by avoiding making long-term attachments with dying patients, I've tried to insulate myself from grief and loss.

Despite this, when Fran asked if I would come back the next day—Christmas Day—I agreed. Harmless enough, I thought. I wasn't scheduled to see patients, but I lived close by, my spouse would be working, and my family was a thousand miles away.

The next morning Daniel answered the door with such a warm smile that I didn't immediately recognize him. This shift in personality reminded me of the time a soft-spoken grandmother threw a plate of eggs at me when I told her that her granddaughter had died. People's normal responses to grief are often anything but normal.

"Kim, it's good to see you. Thanks for coming. Merry Christmas." He reached for my hand with both of his.

A Christmas tree glittered in the foyer and choral music faded in and out of the festive air. Frances was sitting up in bed, smiling with neatly shaded lips, as she cuddled her grandson, Scooter. The chubby, pink infant was tucked in next to his grandmother's body, quietly clutching one of her twiggy fingers. My heart ached at the difference in their faces—one so full of life and one so weary without.

Leslie stood and threw her arms around me. "You're an angel," she whispered into my hair.

I stammered for a moment, explaining that stopping the tube feeds and adjusting her medications was fairly routine. Basic hospice stuff.

Leslie carefully lifted Scooter from the bed. Only after he was clear of his grandmother's frail body did he squirm and flail, like a puppy plucked from play. The family trailed out of the room and Frances and I were left alone.

I asked her about her nausea, her pain, and if she felt hungry. We discussed her energy level, her sleep problems, and some issues with mouth care. After a brief examination, I prepared to leave.

She grabbed my hand. "I want you to be my hospice nurse."

I explained to her that as an admissions nurse, my job was to get all of the administrative things out of the way. She would see her regular nurse in a few days. I didn't go into the fact that I saw my role very clearly— make an instant, intense connection, have one of the hardest conversations of the patient's life, and never see her again. I also didn't mention that it suited me just fine.

"I didn't want to talk about dying, but you changed my mind," she said.

I told her about how busy I was, how overwhelmed the admissions department was by our responsibilities reaching out to people and teaching them about hospice care. "You will love your regular nurse, she is very good."

"But I feel comfortable with you," she said.

"Frances, our department is already understaffed. There are so many families that need our help."

"You told me how close you live. It wouldn't be that much trouble, would it?" I could picture her as the bank executive subtly commanding a room. I couldn't shake the feeling that under different circumstances, we would have been friends.

"Please," she said.

She didn't let me say no. I got permission from my boss to become Fran's hospice case manager, with the agreement that I would still do admissions three days a week.

We started her on several new drugs, including large doses of Dexamethasone. In some ways it was a miracle medication: it decreased pain and nausea, and increased appetite, mood, and energy. But these effects would eventually be overshadowed by negative side effects like agitation, oral thrush, and edema. I carefully explained this was always a temporary fix.

I stopped by most evenings after work and sat with her, to discuss the day's events, the weather, Scooter's progress as he learned to walk. She told me stories about how men treated female bank executives and I added my own tales about egotistical male physicians. We sipped wine like old friends and even when she was tired or sad, her poise impressed me. Sometimes Daniel would storm in, demanding that she needed to rest, and she diffused his anger with a smile. I could picture her quietly, skillfully asserting herself in a raucous business meeting.

One evening I found her sitting in bed, Daniel at her side, with a weary expression. When I asked what was wrong, she burst into tears.

"It's so humiliating." She pressed her hands to her groin.

Cancer treatment to the abdominal region often causes an abnormal passageway, called a fistula, to form between organs. Because of this fistula, a foul-smelling green discharge drained almost constantly from her vagina.

I leaned close to her, especially careful to maintain my composure and respectful non-reactivity, and told her I'd be right back to clean her up. I headed into the bathroom to collect my supplies. So often I wondered if patients knew what they were agreeing to when they chose to pursue aggressive treatments, instead of focusing on quality of life. Our culture encourages patients with a terminal illness to fight to the end, and hospice is often equated with giving up. I'd recently read a study reporting that some patients who chose early hospice care over prolonged aggressive treatment actually lived longer than their non-hospice counterparts. If people knew that much of the life they had left would be plagued by painful and debilitating side effects, would they be so anxious to fight their disease?

On my way back into the bedroom, I paused in the doorway and took in a tender scene. Without the slightest grimace or flinch, Daniel helped her out of her soiled underclothes and wiped her clean. He brought fresh clothes and a pad and tended to his wife with quiet compassion and respect.

During one of my visits the following week, Fran explained that she wanted to go home, to Oklahoma, for one last visit. She was eating solid food for the first time in months, her nausea was gone, her pain was under control. She had energy and a lively spirit. It would be challenging, but she knew what she wanted. We contacted the local hospice in Oklahoma and prepared to discharge her from ours. The airlines required authorization and a doctor's note so that she could travel with her oxygen and medical supplies. She was ecstatic and so was Daniel.

The day before they left I gave them my somber warning lecture. She could get much worse very quickly. She could have a pain crisis on the plane. She could get very confused.

While I spoke, Daniel's face hardened and he wouldn't look at me. When I said she might never make it back to Colorado, he lost it. He leapt from the couch and yanked me up by my arm. I tried to shake him off but his grip was firm. My face burned as he dragged me to the front door and forced me through it, until I was on the landing. He told me never to set foot in the house again.

Before he closed the door Frances was at his side, calm and smiling. She touched his forehead with a tenderness that brought tears to my eyes. I took a slow breath as my anger melted. Maybe I had been too abrupt. There is an art to telling people just exactly as much as they can handle and no more.

She walked me to my car, leaving Daniel inside, and hugged me as I struggled to tamp down my emotions. How could a woman, sentenced to death at such a young age, have no bitterness, no self-pity, and so much compassion for everyone else?

The trip was a success. She saw her family and friends and, although she was tired at times, she told me that she was able to celebrate, eat, drink, engage. For six days after her return she was energetic enough to play with her grandson, to cook with her daughter, and even to go out to eat. Daniel greeted me at the door when I visited, never mentioning his previous outburst. I treated him with distant courtesy.

One week after they returned, my pager beeped early in the morning. The nausea had come back with a vengeance. She couldn't sleep at night and refused to get out of bed during the day. Daniel would find her naked and shivering, but refusing to be covered. Staring at the walls she would cry and call out to her long-dead grandmother. The honeymoon phase of her medication had ended—Frances was delirious.

I knocked on the door. Leslie answered but said nothing. She joined her father who sat on the couch, huddled and staring. I walked past them and into Fran's room.

"Frances?" I whispered into the dark.

I could hear her labored breathing. I walked to her side, placed my hand on her cool forehead. Spit dribbled from her pale, bare lips, forming a crust at the corners. She fluttered her eyelids, acknowledging my presence, but kept them closed. Her chilled hand reached weakly for mine.

"Fran," I whispered. "Are you in pain?"

"Mmmm," she said. "It's today."

"Do you need something for the pain?"

"No." She struggled with a breath. "I don't understand."

"Do you mean you're confused?"

"Maybe confused, but I know it's today."

"Good," I said.

"No. I mean *today*. I will die today."

"Oh, Franny." I put my head close to hers. "Are you ready?"

She drew a haggard breath. "Yes."

Three hours later she was moaning in pain, breaths ragged and wet. I called Dr. Stone, who had maintained a relationship both as an attending physician and a friend. She would be right over.

Lea was short, slim, and fluttery—not your typical cancer doctor. She had a soft voice and gentle demeanor. Cancer doctors were notoriously incompatible with hospice care. Not all of them, of course. Many oncologists moved on to work with hospice, even as they continued fighting cancer with other patients. But, as a group, they generally continued to fight, fight, fight. When hospice was called in, many oncologists felt their job was done, and I'd worked with more than one doctor who acted as though hospice care was medicine's failure.

Even with both Lea and myself at her side, and the family in the living room, Fran could not be comforted. She was in terrible pain "all over," and her breathing was agonizing to listen to. Her once warm brown hair looked faded and brittle.

We needed a different medication, and more of it, to make her comfortable. The house was far from my office and far from any pharmacies. I drove as fast as I could.

When I returned, Daniel had made it to the door of Fran's bedroom. I thought his tight grip on the doorframe might tear it loose. He was crying, hard, but his eyes were dry.

I stepped around him to get into the room.

He grabbed my hand and I instinctively snatched it back. "Do something. Help her," he demanded. Then, "I can't see this." He left.

Frances moaned non-stop, thrashing and pulling at her clothes and sheets. Patients often experience delirium in the final days of life, so much so that we refer to it as terminal delirium. Once it gets rolling it can be very difficult to control.

Lea stood up, looking away. "Let's start an IV and give her 1 milligram of Dilaudid."

"Lea, I'd like to give her three of Versed, too. Should we just give it sub-q?" Instead of having to isolate a vein, subcutaneous injection was given directly into the layer between the fat and skin. Considered old-fashioned and rarely used outside of hospice, sub-q is an easier route than intravenous, both for the patient and the clinician. It would still take effect within minutes.

Lea and I spent most of the day at Fran's bedside. We were able to keep her comfortable, but her pain, delirium, and level of consciousness changed by the minute and her medications needed to be adjusted accordingly.

Finally we got her really relaxed. As she eased in and out of sleep I noticed one of the telltale "six-hour" signs of death—the tip of her nose drooped a little, pulled to the side by gravity.

We convinced Daniel to come into the room and say

good-bye.

He sat next to her, and we stepped into the large adjoining master bathroom to give them some privacy. It had been a long day and we knew it would soon culminate in Fran's death. I had a brief, selfish thought that if I hadn't agreed to be her nurse I wouldn't have to feel this loss.

We were quiet and respectful, but we also needed a break. We began to talk about mundane things—our home lives, gardening, a local restaurant.

We mentioned dinner just as Daniel walked in. His face was clear and calm. He stepped between Lea and me, faced Lea, and touched her shoulder.

"Have you ever been to the Briarwood Inn?" he asked.

She smiled and shook her head.

"It's a beautiful restaurant. Very romantic." His hand trailed down her shoulder to her arm.

She smiled again, looking mildly uncomfortable. I felt like an intruder.

"You know, Lea, I'd really like to take you to dinner sometime."

Fourteen feet from his dying wife, life seeping from her body so rapidly it soured the air, he flirted with her doctor. I stood with my mouth open, fighting the urge to tell him he was a pig. How could he disrespect his beautiful wife so profoundly?

I told myself that responses to grief are as varied as people, and I'd seen some unique manifestations. One family had held hands around the bed of their father, singing and laughing as he took his last breath. The man hadn't eaten in more than a week, and they recounted his notorious love of sweets. When the cot rolled through the door to pick up the body and transport it to the mortuary, the daughter was found stuffing doughnuts into the dead man's mouth.

But I had never seen this before. Maybe Daniel was trying to hold on to the memory of her, of date nights in dimly lit restaurants, his lovely wife happy and healthy. My stomach churned as I tried to make sense of what I saw as his repulsive reaction to a very sad situation.

Lea said nothing for a moment. She leaned back, her eyes red and her brow furrowed. I held my breath, nervous that she would slap him. My heart pounded as I imagined the ugly scene that was about to unfold next to Fran's deathbed. Should I intervene? Lead Daniel out of the room?

But Lea's face relaxed and a tear dripped down her cheek. She took in a deep breath and looked over his shoulder, into the room where her friend lay dying. And with a tenderness I will never forget, she raised her arms and hugged him, gently, the shared pain written in the lines across her forehead.

That's what Frances would have done.

Up Where the Air Is Clear
ANNA EILERTSEN

We were on a walk when my mom first told me she'd started to plan her funeral. It was a short walk to the end of the block and back—one year into cancer, that was as far as she could go. I had been talking about something barely memorable; it had become habit to skirt around the illness and sadness and instead focus on neighbors' gardens and *Orange Is the New Black*. We were almost home when she interrupted me.

"I've been thinking about my service lately. I'll show you where I've started to write down the details, but I want to make sure no one uses the word 'fight' or any of that battle language when they're talking about me."

I would later come to find that the plans she had written down were not just suggestions or ideas, but thoughtful and deliberate arrangements with every detail accounted for. Her wobbly handwriting listed things like the "All Things Bright and Beautiful" processional hymn, Psalm 121 in the *Book of Common Prayer*, the Gospel of Mark 10: 13-16 ("Not typical funeral stuff, but it's my favorite"), a brass band, and a request for no family members to speak at the service ("I just want you to be there").

But that afternoon, she only wanted to talk about the

language. About how the words and metaphors we'd been using to talk about her cancer could actually be playing a part in shaping her experience. I had been so fixated on the reality of the illness itself—on the size of the tumor blocking her bile duct, on the number of cancer spots she had on her liver, on the number of months she had left to live—that the semantics seemed inconsequential.

She continued, "I'm not a fighter and I'm not in a battle. People keep telling me that I am, but those words are too combative. I don't identify with them. I don't like them."

She told me she thought of her cancer as something that had shown up uninvited. She wanted it to leave, she asked it repeatedly to leave, but it had settled in for good. A shitty deal, but a done one. I raised my eyebrows, baffled by her quick-and-tidy rundown of this aggressive, debilitating illness.

"This is not a fight," she said again. "Some days are okay and some days are fucking horrible. Some days, I think about more treatment and some days, I feel ready to die."

Some days, she felt motivated enough to get dressed and leave the house to get lunch and a glass of wine. Some days, she barely left her bed. Many days, I watched her cry as I fiddled with my hands until I thought to bring her a tissue. Her days were barely days at all—they were incidental hours when enough energy could be summoned to hold tight to the railing and walk downstairs. My mom didn't fight these days, she lived them.

It's somehow become a given that cancer is a battle—there are victims, attackers, survivors, and heroes. We are told to fight like hell and use all the weapons at our disposal. Our ability to stand tough against those rapidly dividing cells, to *beat that fucking disease,* somehow becomes tied to our character. People who 'beat' cancer are good people; they are the strong ones, the brave souls whose positivity and determination miraculously work in tandem to conquer this ruthless invader of the body.

But what about the losers, the unlucky, the ones with hidden symptoms and bad timing? If their experience, my mom's experience, is set on a field of battle, then the only option is defeat. My mom's cancer was a struggle every day, but it was not a war. She was unfeigned and resilient, but she was not a fighter. She loved and supported her body and mind until she no longer could.

A few months later, she and I stood in the same place at the end of the driveway, having just returned from an even shorter walk. "Did I ever tell you that I had my palm read once?" She held out her hand, palm up, and pointed to the line running from her thumb to her wrist, her life line.

"I remember the woman saying that I would have an extremely difficult health obstacle...but that I would overcome it." I traced my finger over her life line, knowing this woman was wrong and wishing that willpower, unbridled hope, and the whims of palm readers were enough to keep someone alive.

True to her word, when it was time for my mom to die, she did not fight. On her last morning, her breathing changed from strenuous gasps and grunts to soft breaths, spread apart far enough for us to know they would be her last. Her swift step from life into death was graceful, with no fumbles or false alarms. I watched as she just suddenly stopped living, a memory that can still fill every part of my body and leave me with tears and goosebumps. Not a battle, just a step.

Seeing cancer as a fight is a choice. A choice which certainly helps many people conceptualize their disease. But rejecting that battle does not render someone weak or complicit. Instead, I saw my mother summon a different breed of bravery: the strength to live in the binds of that which constrains you.

At her memorial service, no words of war were spoken. Instead, at her request, a trumpet blasted "Let's Go Fly a Kite," and the packed cathedral did not hesitate to sing.

Your Mother's Place
CINDY E. KING

Already, they have cut her power,
the entire afternoon dies in the butterfly bone
china. A bunch of bananas softens to twilight,
furnishing the apartment with close, sweet air

they are small, brown, tender—
a lost leather glove
fingers curled toward the failing light
around rusting apples, oranges,
tough and wizened,
lemons, bitter,
shrinking into themselves

the last of the grapes resists raisinhood
but blushes, nonetheless, with amber
like clouds in distant city light

relieved of her need to feed us,
the refrigerator stands silent
for the first time in twenty years
warm, dark, newly empty,
fit for stocking with fresh grief

Who Cares for the Care Giver?
SHUBHANGI JOSHI

I watch her,
As she wipes the sweat
Off her brow,
Shivering,
I can hear her trying to
Hide her groaning pain.
Yet,
She kneads and kneads
Till the dough is supple and soft
Enough to feed
A family of four
Waiting impatiently.
I ask,
"Didi, why don't you
Visit a doctor?
You don't look so good."
She says,
"Oh! This?
This is nothing."
As she sweeps her pain
Neatly under the dinner table.
Out of earshot,
And our line of vision.

How to Be a Wife
CATHLEEN CALBERT

In the surgical waiting room, a large woman fell asleep with a large book laid across her chest. The title, in bold letters, was easy for me and everyone else to read: *HOW WE DIE.* I thought about telling her that we die by putting big fat books like that on our big fat chests in places such as this, but I didn't want to tempt any Fates to punish me for behaving badly while my husband underwent disc removal and spinal fusion.

One by one, surgeons came in to talk to families until my own scarlet-clad man beckoned: all went well, an apparent success, hurrah. Several days later, I got to take home my guy: a pain-crazed cup of soup I poured into the car before he parked himself on our couch for good.

Epidural steroid injection. Facet joint injection. Spinal cord stimulation. Radiofrequency medial nerve branch ablation. TENS therapy. Hydrocodone. Morphine. Major surgery. FBS: failed back syndrome.

You think cancer, heart attack, stroke. You don't think back pain is going to take your partner out of the game. Who hasn't had a bad back? I can tell you: no one. How do I know? Because everyone in the world has given me advice to give my husband. He should do acupuncture, get a massage, try meditation, take it easy, take a walk, talk to somebody, how about heat, ice, ibuprofen, herbal teas? Has he tried. Get him to try. Tell him he should try. I feel like I'm the conduit of Man to God, but I guess that would make me the Virgin Mary, and I'm certainly not that.

"Why don't *you* tell him?" I've said to kith and kin, who have looked aghast. They don't want to tell him. They want to tell me. Then they want me to fix him. He's broken: he needs to be fixed! That he remains unwell seems absurd, obstinate, un-American. Although I've told them his ailment is way beyond the usual back problems, friends and family find the idea of something being wrong long-term unacceptable.

It was hard for me, too. I shared frustrations with girlfriends over wine. *If I were in pain....* Although I enjoy commiserating over the obdurate nature of husbands, I felt uncomfortable with that *If I were....* I'd what? Become Joan of Arc all of a sudden? I recalled the urinary tract infections I got back when I had rambunctious sex with my beloved. If I contracted a UTI, I didn't breathe my way through it. I didn't go to yoga and relax into downward dog. I didn't do anything until I got my hands on antibiotics.

In the parlance of such things, I am now a "well spouse." I was reassured to learn on the Well Spouse website that other ill husbands weren't gazing up adoringly all day at their caretaking mates. As pain plunged my guy into the land of the unwell, I'd imagined he would behave more like a character in a sentimental novel: with a shawl over his shoulders and a basin of gruel on his lap, he'd utter thoughtful comments about the vagaries of life and express continual appreciation of his devoted wife. It's hard to hear "bitch" instead of "ministering angel." This epithet from him was unusual but not singular.

"I thank you all the time," he protested, but that day he'd acknowledged the tea and soup, not the dishes or the trash or the laundry or the bills or the long commute to work and back. We continually confound each other. I'm thinking, *How can he not be nice to me, considering all I do for him?* Meanwhile, he's undoubtedly proud of himself for not ripping off my face, then handing it back to me, so I can feel what he feels for once.

Wordsworth wrote, "We Poets in our youth begin in gladness;/But thereof come in the end despondency and madness." Perhaps in marriage it's *What starts with sex ends in nursing.* In our beginning, we couldn't stop touching each other. My lips chafed from continual kissing, I tucked myself into a pastel dress and went to his parents' house for Easter dinner. I wondered then how wanting to bed this boy had led to my putting his mother's ham into my mouth on a religious holiday. Now it's taken me here.

Who needs sex anyway, right? No more UTIs, no danger of STDs. I'm a sealed vessel, a closed fountain. My God, I *am* the Virgin Mary.

My sister said, "This isn't what you signed up for." Except it is. You have to read the contract.

A friend, who also reluctantly turned into a well spouse, warned me, "If there's a wife, everyone will let her do everything." *If there's a wife, there's a way.*

"You're a trooper," my father-in-law told me. I thought, *But am I a lifer?*

A friend said, "You're a saint." I think this means, I don't want to go through what you are. So I don't think I could. Since you can, you must belong to a different category of person than I do. But I'm not a saint. And I've called my ill spouse an asshole.

My brother suggested that at some point I might

need to let him go, that is, commit suicide, the only sure escape from pain like his. I can't imagine what point that would be. When I come downstairs in the morning, I wake my husband with one question: "Are you alive?"

He tells me I've kept him alive. I believe him. Without me, he'd give up and die. Or would he be all right? I've read that those with solicitous spouses report higher levels of pain. I've also read that people experience less pain when they lay eyes on their partners. All I know is that my vision of white-jacketed professionals who'd promptly eradicate my guy's malady derived from TV shows, I'm afraid, not from reality. *Fix him. Why can't you just fix him?*

When my husband first asked his pain management physician to sign off on a form requesting a handicap parking sticker, the doc balked a little. In eloquent but incorrectly inflected English, he said that he didn't want to make him an inVALid. Yes, I thought. An invalid: someone who's null and void. Since then, his doctor has used more terrible words: *incurable, acceptance, disability*.

It's like watching sandcastles as the tide rises: a flag falls, then one turret; finally, the walls of the moat overflow. First, he can't finish painting the kitchen. Then he can't mow the lawn. Then he can't teach anymore. That's when I knew how much pain had eroded his life. Painting a room was one thing. Even going out to dinner to please his wife. But he loved to be in the classroom. This, he didn't want to lose.

"How much are you supposed to do for your partner?" I asked a friend. "Everything," he said. "That's what marriage is. You help each other." I thought, *That sounds ideal, but what does it mean practically?* I also thought, *As a guy, you do EVERYTHING to help your wife? Hmm.* I posted the same question on the Well Spouse message board. The answers I received were supportive but frustratingly Zen. *That's the question you'll keep asking. The answer will keep evolving.*

I know I keep changing. One day, I don't ask if he's eaten *(he must take responsibility for his well-being!)*; the next, I insist he drink cans of liquid protein *(I must take responsibility for his well-being!)*. I fear I'm making a mess of my caretaking: I don't take charge of his life, but he knows I'll step in eventually.

I fear I will become cruel: Baby Jane feeding my housebound husband his own parakeet. I tell myself, *Be kind, Be kind, Be kind.*

I fear if I'm not a good well spouse I will be struck down with my own dread disease. After all, marital caretakers are supposed to have shortened lifespans. I think of Christopher Reeve's super wife, who tended to him until his death, then died of cancer when she should have had thirty years of splendid second-husband sex.

Of course, our lot might be much worse: my husband could be Christopher Reeve. All my hats go off to those taking care of extremely sick and injured loved ones. I don't have to change or bathe my guy. Still, when he told me that he'd prefer to be paralyzed, I said I thought people with paralysis aren't necessarily pain-free, but I wanted to weep over this tall man standing before me wishing he never could do so again if it meant getting rid of his pain.

"Don't be in pain," I say sometimes. It's a dark joke between us. "Why don't you just say no?" When something hurts me, I say, "Don't send your pain my way!"

"Is this our story?" I've asked him, in tears. "Is this how our story ends?"

I've never known how to be a wife.

Certainly, I don't know how to be a wife now that marriage has hit the *worse* part. I remember hearing about this woman who left her husband, whose diagnosis of Stage IV cancer came early in their marriage. She said something like, *It was all about the cancer.* I thought, *Hey, you married him, honey.* Now I think, *Who am I to judge? Who knows what I'd do?* I don't want to hear anymore what people would never do. Wait until they get to never.

In a way, given his dependence, I've gotten what I wanted: a man who will stay with me forever. On the other hand, he leaves me daily, drifting away as far as he can from his painful body. I thought about writing a series of Ghost Husband poems, but this sounds rather depressing. *The apparition of my husband on the couch:/an Easter Lily wilting on the altar....*

I embarrassed him when I, newly in love, swooned over his "Chatterton pale chest" in a poem. A male friend told me I should have balanced this with something about his "Einstein mind," but now I'm glad I celebrated his body when he felt good within it.

More recently, "Painless Villanelle" came from conversations in which I'd said to him, sympathetically, "Nothing trumps pain." In the poem, love does. I believe this can be true in life, too, but I also bow down to the power of pain, which washes away words on the page and the pleasures of touch or talk.

So why write this?

I think of Linda Loman's speech about her failing Willy: "Attention, attention must finally be paid to such a person." At times, I feel I'm the only one who truly sees my husband's distress and decline, that he's only his problem and mine. People give advice and go back to their lives. Yet, we're not alone, I believe, just one of many wounded duos. "Love is all around," The Troggs sang. So is a host of problems that can plunge a couple into contemplating the "in sickness" part of those wedding vows.

I'd proposed to my guy that we write something together: he could describe living with pain, and I could speak to living with *his* pain. I waxed enthusiastic, and he agreed. But he never began. When I asked why, he told me he couldn't stand writing about his condition, though he'd do it "for me." I told him I didn't want him to do it for me. I think we both meant *I still love you.*

Our twentieth wedding anniversary is coming up. We'll get there, if the Fates allow. That's as far ahead as I can see.

Fatherly Fear: To Allen Qing Yuan
YUAN CHANGMING

how much
just how much love should I show you, Son
I do not know, I only know
how I had tried
how I'd persisted in having you as my second child,
  a lifelong companion to your bro
how I had found the greatest joy in merely seeing
  you after each long and hard day
but I never meant for you to have been
36 days prematurely born, and to have begun
Suffering so much when you were only 12 years old,
  suffering
from a terrible drought within your Chinese skin,
  suffering
from bulged disks that cause you to walk like a
  cripple, suffering
from sciatic pain when you move around, suffering
from having to withdraw from your school's
  volleyball team, suffering
from lacking the confidence to emulate your elder
  brother, suffering
from your limitations to kick, jump, run, bend like
  your friends, suffering

from your inability to work outside home to earn
  your own money, oh Son
I do not know, I do not know how much love I
  should show to you:
if a bit too little, you would feel disappointed of my
  fatherly love
if a bit too much, I fear heavens would be so jealous
  as to take you away from me

indeed, how much
just how much love should I show you, Son
I do not know, I only know
after I die, my other self will stand right behind your
  back
wherever you are, whenever there is or there is no
  sunshine
ready to protect you against all evil gods and ghosts

but while still alive, I do not know, Son
how much love I should show you:
if a bit too little, you might feel disappointed of my
  fatherly love
if a bit too much, I fear heavens might be so jealous
  as to take you away from me

This Is How I Heal Him Now
GINA WILLIAMS

I can't help my father, even in my dreams. When he is in trouble or dying in my sleep, I'm never able to reach him in time. Whether he's fallen through a hole in the ice or trapped in a burning car, it's always the same—my outstretched hands cannot get to him, and he won't help himself, his body slouched, face hidden in darkness, arms hanging helplessly at his sides like he's already gone.

My dad is so overweight now that he has to hold on to things when he moves around the house. His legs are often swollen with fluid. He's taking three or four different blood pressure drugs and cholesterol medication that makes his muscles burn. His feet ache constantly. His ankles turn inward when he stands from the weight of his body. An entire cupboard in his kitchen is filled with pills. For years now, he's had to hook himself up to a mess of hoses and straps I call the "snore machine" for his severe sleep apnea. He can no longer tell the difference between side effects and real sickness.

My attempts to help him in real life have never amounted to anything, either.

"Maybe you should try swimming," I said one day, trying to sound casual and easygoing. He was having trouble walking and breathing. He'd gained even more weight since I saw him last.

He didn't look away from the enormous flat-screen television in front of his overstuffed recliner. It was halftime during a Denver Broncos football game, and a loud commercial was blaring through the room.

"Yeah right, Big Al the whale. Maybe they could train me to do tricks for food," he said, reaching for the remote.

He turned up the volume.

"I'm serious, Dad. You could swim year-round, and the pool is right up the street."

He didn't respond and pulled the handle on his recliner, pushing his swollen legs into the air. He was wearing shorts in December, white socks, and blue orthotic-looking sandals.

I'd previously told him about a hypnotist I went to for my water fear. It helped me so much that I thought he might want to try it for weight loss.

"Did you call the hypnotist?"

"Yeah, the guy wanted seventy-five bucks a visit," he said. "Can you believe that? What, so he can make me eat like a bird—and probably cluck like a chicken, too? Seventy-five bucks! That's eight bacon cheeseburgers and a six pack—with change!"

I felt my face flush. I stopped myself from asking him if he'd priced the cost of a funeral lately. I stopped myself from saying, "Don't you love me enough to need me as much as I need you?"

I watched his chest rise and fall with heavy breaths and wanted to cry and hold him and slap him all at once. I swore then that I would never talk to him about his health again.

"You worry too much," he said when I got ready to leave. "Besides, at this rate you won't ever have to put me in an old folks home."

. . .

I've had an irrational fear of my dad dying for so long I can't remember *not* worrying about it, even when he was healthy. I wonder if I sensed all that time ago what was coming—that life would beat him down, and he'd stop fighting back, that I'd spend most of my adult years trying to help him, that the last time we'd ever hike together in the mountains was when I was sixteen years old.

One night, when I was maybe six or seven, my dad made good on a promise to take me on a midnight call, the emergency radio crackling on his nightstand. I was still in my footie pajamas when he lifted me into his tow truck. "Just a fender bender," he'd said. I bounced with excitement all the way to the scene, out of my mind with excitement about being part of his mysterious and important job.

But the headlights revealed a terrifying mangle, a hologram of blood and shattered glass. "Aw geez, don't look," he said, and got to work, the flashers illuminating him in pulsing loops. He looked too small against the wreck, his breath twisting in the beams as I waited inside the dark cab, holding onto the steering wheel. I stood up on the seat and put my fingers on the windshield. My curiosity was crushed. I felt afraid for him, sorry. With one eye squeezed shut I could create the illusion of touching him, and I imagined maybe he could feel the warmth of my fingertip on his cheek, that maybe I could get him back inside that way, pull him out of the mess, away from danger.

My parents married when they were still teenagers. Dad went on one final overseas tour on an aircraft carrier during the Vietnam War after I was born, and then his military career was over. He'd planned to go back to school and become an officer, but my mom was young and afraid with a baby at home and begged him not to re-enlist.

By the early 1980s, he'd saved up enough from his mechanic's wages to buy a gas station, then a second, and a third. I think he was almost as happy then as he had been sailing around the world. But the oil companies began pushing out independent owners. They tripled his rent and forced him to sell or be a company man. He started over digging ditches on a county work crew.

In my memory, the fatal blow came when he gave up his dream to own his own business. He'd come home at the end of those long days out in the elements, exhausted physically and mentally, slump in his chair, and not speak to anyone. He looked blank, broken. All of his edges sagged. His weight started to climb.

• • •

If there is any good in all of this, it might be that my dad's lack of motivation helps fuel mine. I am not a natural-born distance runner. I'm small and compact, built of fast-twitch muscle fibers. But my psyche is somehow better suited for distance, for pushing limits and testing boundaries, and I crave long, solitary moments when my mind can separate from a body in motion. I feed off the powerful feeling that comes from having the kind of discipline it takes to train my body to do difficult things.

For several years now, I have entered a weekend-long relay race that goes from the Cascade Mountains to the Oregon coast. My favorite stretch is always the midnight leg through the foothills. I think about my dad often when I'm out running or cycling. I can't talk to him about his health anymore. There's no real outlet for my grief and fear. So this—pumping my own heart and pushing my own limits on midnight runs—this is how I heal him now.

I thought about him intensely one night out there during my section of the relay. I set out alone in the darkness on a gravel mountain road deep in the coastal forest, working my muscles and lungs into a smooth rhythm and easing into a fast, steady, meditative pace. Step-step-step, breathe. Step-step-step, breathe. After a quarter mile, my legs and lungs and arms were perfectly synced. Step-step, breathe. Step-step, breathe. I floated through the night in that rhythm, landing softly, relaxing into my stride, suspended in that perfect place where time becomes itself, where getting somewhere no longer matters.

I pictured my dad at home as I ran, dozing in his chair in front of the television or maybe in bed hooked up to his apnea machine, his lungs laboring against the weight of his enormous belly. I imagined then that I could breathe for him, that the air in my lungs became his, and if he could feel this again, even for a moment, it would make him want it back. I became so focused on breathing for him that I felt lifted outside of myself, and it was him running on that road instead of me, his healthy body in motion, racing through the night.

See, Daddy-O, I thought as we leaned into a hill, pushed higher. *Don't tell me this doesn't feel good. This is the good hurt. This is you, this is you. The good hurt is never too late.* I wanted to slash open a hidden vein right then, stop my dad's long, slow suicide, pour myself and my fight, the fight he gave me, back into him right there on the gravel.

We ran together like that for miles, smooth as starlight with animal fluidity, our bodies filled with pure energy and strength instead of bones and guts. We ran until I could hear cowbells in the distance, could see headlamps through the trees, the end of my segment around the next bend, but as the finish line neared, he faded away in the commotion, slipped away, disappeared the way ghosts do, into the night.

San Pablo Avenue
JUDY JUANITA

Is San Pablo Avenue still the longest street in Northern California? we drive down this old wide Oakland street, my father, his walker and I, out and about. it's a nice day, a good day. we pass his haunts: the key club, the hotel California, the social club, the oaks club. I wonder as he looks at them, his gambling joints, a faint smile on his long face, I wonder: is daddy ready to go?

does he see what I see as I drive down this bygone path? does he see what the pawnshop gobbled like a wolf, hungry and salivating outside the door? bicycles, the huge console television, plastic transistor radios, the iron. does he see me heating the heavy cast iron on the stove and scorching my white blouse every time? the wolf wanted everything we could give it, just everything, even a house gambled away in all-night poker.

we pull up to the temple in a town beyond San Pablo. he chants with me at home. I want him to chant with me here. we pull into the long driveway. my father lifts a weak leg out when two young men politely try to help. they begin to pull and tug him out of the car and all at once he decides he's not going. we've driven all this way, past every sordid, boarded-up, closed-down, gone-to-seed, burnt-to-the-ground landmark of his gambling years. I want this redemption for him but he'll have none of it. his jaw sets and he mutters *don't try to push your religion down my throat.*

I get bubbling boiling cauldron-in-my-chest mad. I go inside and chant while he sits in the car and listens to jazz. I want redemption all right. I want everything. just everything and I want it for me. I want the bicycles back, the televisions, the radios, the iron, the white blouses, and all the moments, each and every one, before the wolf began to blow the house down.

after I chant I feel better. but it takes a while. we drive back down San Pablo Avenue. he looks around with the exact same expression, the same faint smile. we pass Golden Gate Fields, the big clock next to the freeway (post time: 1 p.m.). I slow down as we pass the grandstand. it demands that of me, of us. it is empty and quiet. but as we pass I hear the announcer's nasal staccato, the horses' hooves pounding the sod, the crowds jumping out of their seats, the sigh of the losers, the brash laugh, all of a kind, from the winners. I see him, his hair black and curly and trimmed just so, his moustache black and full. I smell his chewed-up cigar, watch him handicap the daily double and fold the racing form under his arm. as clear as the trumpet's call to the post, I hear his *hey buddy, whatcha know good.*

The Outing

STEPHANIE WAXMAN

You wait for the light to turn green. The air smells like rain. The light changes. Hurry, but be careful. The wheels of the walker catch in a pothole. Lift it up and quickly, quickly...cars so close with their heavy rumbles, urging you faster...the light now yellow and you're only halfway. Your bladder gives up and you can feel the diaper getting heavy. Cars zip behind you. The first raindrops touch your head as you lift the walker onto the curb.

Take a moment, catch your breath. A spray of birds explodes like confetti against the gray sky, as if to applaud your triumph. You remember the day Ted took Charlie duck hunting. How worried you were that he was too young to join the killing game that men seem to love. And then, the excitement on his face when he dragged in the bird for you to see, Ted shaking his head and smiling with an I-told-you-so look.

It is sprinkling. If you catch cold it will turn to pneumonia and then you will go to the hospital again. Wheel forward quickly. Your head is getting wet. Hurry into the 7-Eleven. You cross the threshold and a buzzer makes a loud sound. The man behind the counter is new. He is a Jap. You must not think of him this way; they are not our enemy now. Hurrying has made you tired, so very tired. He comes over and offers you a chair. You look faint, he says. It is a folding metal chair. How will you get up from such a flimsy thing? But you are tired, and if you fainted here, they would take you to the hospital. So you hold onto the walker, hoping it will not roll away when you tip back to sit. The Jap holds the chair as you fall heavily downward. There. You are sitting. You can take a moment, catch your breath.

He is handing you a can of soda and talking about his mother. Your hand shakes, but you swallow from the can. The sting of the bubbles enters your nose. Some of the soda gets down your blouse, into your brassiere. The soggy diaper gives off a sour smell. You would like to be home, dry and warm. You would like to be in bed watching Oprah.

The man is asking you something. His face is only inches from yours. His teeth are stained and his breath stinks of garlic. Is there someone he could call? You don't know the neighbors yet. Charlie is teaching seventh graders in a community you have never heard of. The Jap is asking, should he call a taxi? He wants to call a taxi to take you home. He wants you to leave now.

You do not have any money because the bank machine was broken. You cannot pay for a taxi. You cannot pay for this soda. And the soda has made your bladder full again. No, you tell him, and thank you for the chair, the soda. He helps you up, his garlic breath covering you, talking about his mother and taxis and the weather. You look outside and see that it has stopped raining. You can make it if it is not raining.

Roll the walker right through the puddles. You feel angry again about the broken bank machine. Now you will have to wait until Sunday, when Charlie comes with the groceries and petty cash. And you will have to wait until he leaves before you can go out for cigarettes, since he would get angry if he knew you still smoked. A whole generation of people who don't smoke. You think of that red package of Pall Malls always sticking out of Ted's shirt pocket. You remember sitting together on the porch, drinking scotch rocks and smoking Pall Malls. Then, inside, onto the bed. His mouth on your skin.

Your shoes rub against your swollen feet and if your feet get wet, you will catch your death…you hear your mother warning you. It has been a long time since you have thought of her and now you can imagine her voice and her words, but you cannot remember how she looked that day when it rained so much and your feet got wet and she took your temperature. You cannot remember if she was wearing glasses then. You can only remember her as she was at the end, an old woman lying in a hospital, her faded hair on the pillow.

You see the apartment. Suddenly, you do not want to go inside, into the cramped space that Charlie has chosen for you. You think of your house in Glendale with its rolling lawn and wide driveway. You remember Ted playing basketball with Charlie in the summer and how the thump against the wall boomed into the kitchen. You would bring out lemonade and sit under the sycamore and marvel that Ted could keep up, now that Charlie was so tall.

You face the steps. There is something on the railing, a soggy rag or maybe a handkerchief. It is trimmed in red. Maybe it's silk. Tuck it inside your pocket. Now, fold the walker. With your other hand, pull yourself up and be careful to hold tight. One more step and…push open the door and lean the walker against the wall. Close the door and hold onto the table until you reach your chair. Collapse onto it. Here you are, you made it. It is warm and smells of cinnamon and coffee.

The clock and the refrigerator hum together.

You need to get out of these shoes and socks. You need to get a new diaper. But first, take a moment. Catch your breath. You remember the little red-edged scarf. You take it from your pocket and smooth it out on your lap. In the middle, there is a dragon in front of a mountain. All around the mountain, there are drawings of naked people. Each little drawing shows a naked man and a naked woman bending this way and that, tangled together. You turn the scarf over and see the writing: *48-WAYS*. You study the little figures again, the naked men and women. Forty-eight ways to screw! Yes, that's it! There are forty-eight different ways to screw and each one is displayed on this silky scarf! Oh, how you wish you could show this to Ted. Wouldn't he get a kick out of it. For the first time today you laugh, laugh so hard tears come and you feel your diaper filling again. But this time, it doesn't bother you. The very fact of it makes you laugh harder.

Hospital Poems
SARAH FELDMAN

Hospital poems…weak—without skill or perseverance; only managing to beat their wings softly
— *"Ellen West" by Frank Bidart*

I.

I am not myself. Days pass; I write them off.

I sit in the sun. Spring comes, knuckle by knuckle,
buds pressing out, dogwood blooming in white fists.

Walks in the courtyard, watched over by a dull
    inquisitor
who asks, over and over, one question, always
    unanswerable, *Where*
does it hurt?

Pain is elsewhere—in the face of my inquisitor,
endlessly patient, scrupulously blank,
in the shuffle of the old man who goes so slow
in his daily crossing of the grass, his whole being
distilled into the ache and heft
of one more step.

Or else what? There is nothing left to write off.
Worse days are coming. Gather up your bed.

. . .

II.

I lost a spring—thrush song, the smell of rain-bitten
    earth,
white buds expunged from their sockets, Northern
    Cross
swinging back up over the horizon—I would like to
    say
I felt these things through some other sense, as a
    winter bulb
feels the weak February sun through six inches of
    earth,
hears, through the clamped cell of its own body,
the thunder of spreading tendrils, the other seeds
    awakening, breaking into sunlight,
as a deaf man hears music in the bones of his feet
    and the roots of his teeth.

No, I don't think so. I lost count—a spring, a
    summer,
getting better, getting worse—the same view from
    the bedroom window,
the light holding in the white lanterns of the mock
    orange, or vanishing
into its deep green folds; the same waste.

I measured out my days in the compartments of
    plastic pill organizers:
one light blue to chase off the fog on waking
three pink to blur the impassable hours of sunlight

two dark blue to lay waste the night
and the three white stones, that made me sick and
    stupid and thick and blank,
to build a bridge back to my life.

Only sometimes my hands shook, reaching for the
    bottle
to dole out the daily stones.

Only sometimes the old lust returned—
the days killed piecemeal in pink or white or blue
    oblivion,
the days to come still round and whole and uselessly
    intact
like bright fruits bred to rot on the vine—
to take all that waste together, and swallow.

· · ·

III.

Do you feel pain?

How easily the skin repairs itself,
the yellow and red fibers busily re-crossing the gap
like pine needles knitting back into themselves
after some riffling of the air.

Do you feel pain?

My body slumped before me at the kitchen table,
a winter vegetable, well-stocked with dense white
    flesh.

Are you safe?

Later, when the blood I almost hadn't believed in
came, red and rich and so much of it
twisting rivulets over my arms stomach legs,
I dreamed, for the first time in years, of water—
rivers leading out over the hidden waterfall to the
    unknown sea.

Are you safe?

· · ·

IV.

Is this the bottom? But there's no rest here.
Each morning you make again your sleepless bed,
folding clean sheets over the narrow strait
where you twist each night as on a grill.

Breakdown? What is that? Each morning you tie
    back your hair
and walk the halls. Under the long, bleared windows
    of the dayroom
you sit blinking and peeling an orange. You sit you
    stand answer
to your name when called, still bent
whole under the gestures that broke you.

The strong, blank sunlight floods the dayroom.
Above the brick-and-glass complex, a perfect
    summer blue—
cloudless, without secrets. There's nothing for you
    there.
Beyond the concrete horizon, it all leaks away,
and whatever it is you wanted—
an extra sleeping pill, some new song
to get you through the night—is nowhere.

Letter to a Newborn Poet
JULIA OLDER

My Dear Elizabeth Fremont,

I was sorry to read that you are bedridden. In your last letter, you write, "I don't know whether to put myself completely at the mercy of the doctor." I suppose the same can be said for the advice of any expert, whether a physician or creative writing professor. All the patient or writer can do is listen and consider the alternatives. We enter a 'room of one's own' to develop a 'mind of one's own.'

I've often suspected that illness seeks the pupating poet inert in the moist wings of the chrysalis, hesitant to enter a new world of creativity. We withdraw into a dark room, climb into bed, and succumb to the oversolicitous care of family members and authoritative doctors.

I once happened on a book exploring the psychological impact of illness on celebrated authors and their writing. The example I most vividly recall is the French memoirist Marcel Proust, who suffered from severe asthma.

While writing *Remembrance of Things Past,* he paneled his room with cork to deafen the Paris street noise and dwelt within like aging wine stoppered in a bottle.

Suffering chronic insomnia from daily asthma attacks and nightly coughing fits, he swaddled himself in blankets and, bolstered on a mountain of pillows, wrote and slept in bed. Around midnight, he would dine at a nearby bistro or, when too ill, would have dinner delivered to his room. Once, when invited to stand at a friend's wedding, Monsieur Proust arrived wearing so many heavy wool sweaters and coats, he could not walk down the aisle and was forced to use a side entrance to join the bride and groom at the altar.

It's laughable, yet edifying, to think how he carried his environment with him like a turtle in its shell. Sickness can be a sage teacher whose lessons surreptitiously seep into us, body and soul. Whether or not there's a connection between Proust's insular personality and chronic bouts of asthma-induced insomnia, he did get a lot of writing done in his cork-insulated room.

If parents or partners don't recognize the signs that you aren't who you were, Elizabeth, it's up to you to take charge, even (especially) as you let go and yield to fatigue. Best to 'go away' the others and entertain morbid thoughts, feverous remorse, torment, confusion and weakness alone. Above all, listen and wait in that twilit catching-caught state of turmoil and twisted sheets.

Did Coleridge's muse—the 'divine ventriloquist'—speak through you? Try to jot down feverish visions and dreams, and while you are convalescing, review them. The new you is capable of fresh insights and interpretations of the subconscious ideas filling your notebook.

Being an invalid is not an option. No one is *invalid* unless she or her beloved sees herself as such. Elizabeth Barrett Browning's family considered her an invalid—

until she met Robert and wrote her *Sonnets from the Portuguese*.

Sometimes, what we need more than anything is reCREATION. Many think that daydreaming and lollygagging around are the same as being lazy and unproductive. How little they know of the creative spirit. The space of carefree days spent swimming, walking, sleeping, reading and not thinking overly much both nurtures and directs us toward an inner vision beyond mere *pursuits*.

· · ·

To be a *convalescent* means to grow in valor or strength. Here again, Ms. Fremont, I'm reminded of how you used this word only in the context of your illness, not realizing that those who live life to the fullest are perennial convalescents seeking health of body and spirit.

Recovery can be sweet if you let it. Repose with the blinds drawn for SLOW re-entry. It is difficult to embrace a new life (or any life at all) when we are body-worn and hounded by the 'musts' and 'shoulds' of overbearing souls.

Allow yourself to build your strength on the reserves of others. You owe them nothing but gratitude. And what do you owe yourself? A new courageous life (once you are well) outside the cocoon they would keep you in. Illness often is precipitated by a depleted energy or volition to proceed. If you are reluctant to tell duty-bound outsiders "I won't" or "I can't," try the conditional "I might," or "I might not." Saying "no" is a good prerogative, too. Open doors. Fly, drive, ride away. Vacate (the root of that wonderful word *vacation*). Be alone in a crowd, but not lonely. Talk to others and be aware of what they and you say. Keep a travel journal, not necessarily to record where you have been, but the people you met, the smiles or altercations, the pulse of thoughts coming and going. Trust your instincts and what you've already learned, perhaps as recently as this illness.

I cannot say I am immune to depression, and I doubt anyone truly is. But those with inner private lives of an expressive nature are subject to troughs of despair. Most people conform and learn coping defenses that seem like second nature to them. Poets, however, are like baby violets that have been uprooted, trampled and kicked aside. Only detachment allows them to regenerate stronger roots, flower and produce essence.

My own peculiar hang-up has been to promote the sacred trust of poetry. In doing so, I may have introduced self-doubts and stalled the natural momentum and direction of your newly-hatched manuscript. This wasn't my intent. Still, doubt can be a positive motivation for assessing poetry.

Do you know the word *credo*? The credo poem usually manifests early, and then it often goes unrecognized. Later poems may be admired and even published for their technique, wit and trendy style or form. They become what is known as 'signature poems' because of their popularity with the public. But early, lyrical poems often continue to seep through our pores—they are the key that unlocks who we are. Most amazing, these seed-wings of maturation reappear as landmark credo poems in our lifelong walkabout.

I was told to keep all poems, and pass that advice on to you. The unschooled poem may be messy, idiosyncratic and not what your friends want to read or hear—but it's yours.

What I'm trying to convey, Elizabeth, is that the sustained clarity and outgrowth of vision gained from experience will eventually coalesce, revealing a hidden universe—sometimes felicitous, sometimes swirling through the dark current of the collective conscious.

All of us wallow in what we think has been inflicted upon us. But if we are patient, unlike others, we have our poems to light the way, and maybe even lead a few lovesick souls with us through the dark wood.

Take it easy. Coraggio!
Julia (Older)

Discussion Questions

1. Was there a moment in this book when you found
    your expectations about gender or illness
    "uprooted"? Did you discover any new perspectives
    on what it means to be a partner, parent, or adult
    child when health states are in flux?

2. Several authors, including Amy Berkowitz, Cathleen
    Calbert, and Karen Land, wrote their stories in
    fragments as opposed to one linear narrative. How
    were you affected by this narrative structure as a
    reader? Was it jarring? Confusing? Moving?
    Frustrating? Familiar?

3. Leah Givens, author of "The Cruelest Month," was
    trained as a neurologist before migraines put an end
    to her pursuit of medicine. Did her character's
    medical authority affect your evaluation of her story?

4. In "The Protective Mundane" Jayinee Basu writes,
    "My body can bury its trauma peculiarly well and
    this scares me. A person without the memories of
    their formation is not a person." What is the trauma
    that Basu buries? What does her character feel is lost

when her body buries its trauma, and how does this loss relate to her suicidal impulses?

5. Annie Dawid writes in "All Thy Waves" about the psychological impact of the Columbine shooting during her pregnancy. Was there a time in your life when an external event significantly impacted your mental, emotional, physical, or spiritual health?

6. In "My Seaweed Chest," author Leonore Hildebrandt touches upon the way sexuality is overlooked in medicine. Have you had a health care experience in which you felt your sexuality was silenced, shamed, excluded or simply ignored? Have you had positive health care experiences around sexuality?

7. Many *Uprooted* characters wrestle with the divide between how they feel and how they are seen in the world. Have you ever felt that you had to pass as something that didn't feel true to your own identity? For example, have you had to pass as happy, or healthy, or straight, or white?

8. In "Up Where the Air Is Clear," author Anna Eilertsen's mother wants to "'make sure no one uses the word "fight" or any of that battle language'" when talking about her cancer. Why does she make this request? Do other *Uprooted* pieces reveal a different relationship to battle metaphors?

9. In "Hospital Poems," author Sarah Feldman italicizes the lines "Do you feel pain?" and "Are you safe?" Other writers, including Stephanie Waxman and Erin Bertram, also break the fourth wall. Does

the second-person perspective change how you relate to the narrator?

10. Are there any characters in *Uprooted* who you believe were judged or treated unfairly based on health status, perceived health status, abilities or limitations?

11. Consider a time, either in this book or in your own life, when a health experience resulted in more than one choice about how to proceed, and you or someone else had to make a decision. How did different kinds of authority (for example, patient experience, scientific objectivity, or the medical hierarchy) influence that decision?

12. Who or what do you think is underrepresented or misunderstood in this book? Can you think of barriers that prevent certain stories from being voiced and shared?

Writing Prompts

"This Is How I Heal Him Now," by *Uprooted* writer Gina Williams, began as a private letter to the author's father. Williams says that although reading the piece did not impact her father's lifestyle, "I do believe my outreach and 'therapy' through writing did help me let go and create some healing space between us."

Like Gina, we believe art can heal. But creative self-expression can be difficult, and open communication about gender and illness in your own life can be particularly challenging. For many people, one of the biggest barriers is just knowing where to begin. To that end, here are some writing prompts from our authors that may help you get started.

1. Imagine your body is an environment. Situate it in a location and time. What is the atmosphere like? Is it more like a conference hall or a planet? Is there a conflict occurring or is it at peace? Who inhabits this environment?

    — *Jayinee Basu*

2. Write about a journey (long or short) that you've taken that included some kind of transformational

change (big or small).
— *Stephanie Waxman*

3. In "The Things They Carried," Tim O'Brien writes, "They carried all the emotional baggage of men who might die. Grief, terror, love, longing—these were intangibles, but intangibles had their own mass and specific gravity, they had tangible weight." Consider a time of illness, grief, caregiving, change, or trauma. Make a list or lists of the physical and emotional items carried during that time.
    — *Gina Williams*

4. Recall an experience when you have interacted with someone in poor physical or mental health. Write down a paragraph describing the scene in the third person. Now rewrite the scene in first person, assuming the patient's perspective. How might they have felt about you, the caregiver, during that time of their crisis or illness?
    — *Gina Williams*

5. Find a time when you are not emotionally charged or in a period of intense struggle. In that moment, write a letter to yourself for future times of struggle. What would you like to hear? What do you think would help?
    — *Andrea Freund*

Contributors

ASAD ALVI is a writer from Karachi, Pakistan. He has conducted and facilitated several fiction writing workshops at Open Letters, a growing society of writers and artists. In 2014, he was accepted to the Young Writers Workshop at Lahore University of Management Sciences. His work has been published in a collection of short stories entitled *I'll Find My Way* (Oxford University Press, 2014), launched at the 5th Karachi Literature Festival, and in an international anthology of contemporary poems, *We Will Be Shelter* (Write Bloody Publishing, 2014). He writes about issues of gender and sexuality to voice opinions on subjects that remain a taboo in patriarchal Pakistani society. Art, Alvi believes, is the most effective tool to bring about awareness, and thus, social change.

JOAN ANNSFIRE is a writer, poet and retired librarian who lives in Berkeley, California. Her poetry chapbook, *Distant Music*, was published by Headmistress Press in 2014. Following her cancer diagnosis, Annsfire began to write as though her life depended on it. Her poetry has appeared in many anthologies and literary journals, including *The Times They Were A-Changing: Women*

Remember the 60s & 70s, *Milk and Honey*, *The Other Side of the Postcard*, *The Queer Collection*, *The Cancer Poetry Project Anthology*, *99 Poems for the 99 Percent*, Counterpunch *Poets' Basement*, *Lavender Review*, *Poetry Superhighway*, *OccuPoetry*, *SoMa Literary Review*, *Harrington Lesbian Literary Quarterly*, *Sinister Wisdom*, *13th Moon*, *Bridges* and *The Evergreen Chronicles*. Her stories can be found in *Identity Envy* and *Sinister Wisdom*. Annsfire was also an award-winning guest contributor to the online community forum A Simple Revolution, sponsored by Aunt Lute Books.

A San Francisco-based writer, JAYINEE BASU is the author of a book of poems entitled *Asuras* (Civil Coping Mechanisms, 2015) and has written for a wide variety of publications. She graduated from UC San Diego with BAs in Political Science and Literature/Writing, as well as a minor in Studio Art. She is a volunteer research assistant at the Memory and Aging Center at UCSF, where she aids research in neural network functions and frontotemporal dementia. Basu is also currently finishing a pre-med program at UC Berkeley.

AMY BERKOWITZ is the author of *Tender Points*, published this year by the Oakland, California, small press Timeless, Infinite Light. She's also the author of two chapbooks, *Listen to Her Heart* (Spooky Girlfriend, 2012) and *Lonely Toast* (what to us, 2010). Her writing has appeared in *580 Split, Dusie,* and *Where Eagles Dare*, and on the VIDA blog. In 2014, Berkowitz was a writer-in-residence at Alley Cat Bookstore & Gallery. She currently lives in a rent-controlled apartment in San Francisco, which serves as the headquarters of her small press, Mondo Bummer Books, as well as the venue for Amy's Kitchen Organic Reading Series. From her own experience as a woman living with chronic pain in a culture that generally mistrusts both female testimony and the concept of invisible illness, Berkowitz has developed deep insights about illness and gender, as well as a righteous anger that she enjoys channeling into her writing. She believes that breaking the silence around the underrepresented crises that emerge at the intersection of illness and gender is the only way to resolve them, and she takes great pleasure in doing so.

GINA MARIE BERNARD writes and lives in Bemidji, Minnesota, where she teaches high school English. She is a tattooed blocker for the Babe City Rollers roller derby team, and claims that her daughters, Maddie and Parker, are the two halves of her heart. Bernard's work has recently appeared or is forthcoming in *Appalachia*, *Balloons Lit. Journal*, *The Bat Shat*, *Border Crossing*, *Cimarron Review*, and *Fox Cry Review*.

ERIN M. BERTRAM is a PhD student and Teaching Assistant in Creative Writing at the University of Nebraska-Lincoln, an OutSpeaking volunteer with the campus LGBTQA+ Resource Center, and winner of the 2016 Karen Dunning Scholarly Paper/Creative Activity Award from the Women's & Gender Studies Department for the lyric hybrid text manuscript "It Is Not a Lonely World." The author of *Memento Mori* (2014) and ten other chapbooks, Erin has received awards from the Frank O'Hara Chapbook Series, Prague Summer Program for Writers, and the Academy of American Poets, with work appearing in *Diagram*, *Leveler*, *So to Speak*, and elsewhere. Erin is a Zen practitioner, holds an MFA from Washington University in St. Louis as a former Teaching Fellow, and has led creative writing and LGBTQ ally workshops for a variety of organizations.

CATHLEEN CALBERT's writing has appeared in many publications, including *The New Republic, The New York Times,* and *The Paris Review.* She has published three books of poetry: *Lessons in Space* (University Press of Florida, 1997), *Bad Judgment* (Sarabande Books, 1998), and *Sleeping with a Famous Poet* (WordTech Communications, 2007). Her fourth book, *The Afflicted Girls,* won the Vernice Quebodeaux Poetry Prize and is forthcoming from Little Red Tree Publishing. Calbert has also been awarded *The Nation*'s Discovery Prize, a Pushcart Prize, and the Mary Tucker Thorp Award from Rhode Island College, where she is currently a professor of English. She, like many, became a 'well spouse' when her husband became disabled by chronic pain. "How to Be a Wife" expresses the confusion of how to take on this role and how to be a caretaker.

KIMBERLY A. CONDON graduated from the University of Wisconsin-Madison and has spent twenty years in the field of medicine, both as a nurse and as a paramedic. Her previous work has been included in the anthology *I Wasn't Strong Like This When I Started Out* (Gutkind, 2013) and published by *Slate.*

ANNIE DAWID's three books of fiction have been published by commercial, university and literary presses, in that order. She is raising her now fifteen-year-old son in Monument, Colorado, where she teaches creative writing and tutors. Her current plan is to attend a history-literature program at Cambridge University when her son leaves for college. Since her experience of severe depression during pregnancy in 1998-99, the subject of pregnant women's mental health has come to the fore, and is now included in pre- and postnatal healthcare.

ANNA EILERTSEN studied English at Whitman College and now lives in Oakland, California. Her mother's journey with cancer sparked an interest in the experience of illness and, specifically, how language plays a part in shaping that experience. Eilertsen knows first-hand that harnessing a sense of humor through writing lends an incredible ability to help us endure illness and heal from the wrack and ruin it often leaves. She believes that good cheese and whiskey sours are also quite helpful.

DANA FASCIANO received her MFA in poetry from Chatham University in 2008. Her work has appeared in various print and online publications including *Black Book Press, Lunarosity*, and *The Working Poet: 75 Writing Exercises and a Poetry Anthology* (Autumn House Press, 2009). She was also the recipient of the 2008 Laurie Mansell Reich Poetry Prize. Illness and gender are two topics that are very close to the author and much of her writing addresses themes of eating disorders, body image, and sexuality. Having struggled with anorexia herself many years ago, she feels that it is important to shed light on the many facets of this often misunderstood disease. Fasciano currently teaches writing at Rutgers University.

SARAH FELDMAN's poems have been published in *The New Quarterly, The Malahat Review, The Antigonish Review, Dandelion, Grain, Fiddlehead, Pacifica Literary Review*, and *One Throne Magazine*. Several of her poems also appeared in the anthology *Undercurrents: New Voices in Canadian Poetry* (Cormorant Books, 2011). Feldman is a dual citizen of the United States and Canada, and her imaginative landscape draws on both coastal British Columbia and the Connecticut River Valley. Currently a resident of Springfield, Massachusetts, Feldman teaches English and Latin at Commonwealth Academy. She wrote "Hospital Poems" as a way of comprehending a time in her life when both illness and its cures seemed to make it impossible for her to ever recover her own voice.

ANDREA FREUND is a graduate of Stanford University, where she received her BS in biology. She currently works in technology communications as a copywriter, marketer, and user researcher. Born and raised in Texas, Andrea now calls San Francisco's Haight Ashbury neighborhood home. Outside of work, Andrea dabbles in fiction and humor writing. She's also an avid runner, questionable dancer, and aggressive Scrabble player.

LEAH GIVENS is a member of the St. Louis group Writers Under the Arch. Her work has appeared in *The Citron Review*, *The Healing Muse*, and the *Yale Journal for Humanities in Medicine*, among others. She received her MD from Washington University in St. Louis. Since the time chronic migraines led her to resign from her position at an Alzheimer's research center, she has developed an increased interest in communicating the experience of having migraines and her involvement with new research and treatment options.

LEONORE HILDEBRANDT is the author of a letterpress chapbook *The Work at Hand* (Flat Bay Press/Stone Island Press, 2011) and a full-length collection titled *The Next Unknown* (Pecan Grove Press, 2014). She has published poems and translations in *The Cafe Review*, *Cerise Press*, *Cimarron Review*, *Denver Quarterly*, *Drunken Boat*, *The Fiddlehead*, and *Poetry Salzburg Review*. Winner of the 2013 Gemini Poetry Contest, she has received fellowships from the Elizabeth George Foundation, the Maine Community Foundation, and the Maine Arts Commission. Her work has been nominated twice for a Pushcart Prize. A native of Germany, Hildebrandt lives "off the grid" on the coast of Maine, where she teaches writing at the University of Maine and serves as an editor for the *Beloit Poetry Journal.* To her, the body's fragility seems both marvelous and unsettling. In times of illness, a sense of integrity is easily lost. To write poetry offers solace—crafting language into something musical; a way of saying, "I am here."

JANIS BUTLER HOLM lives in Athens, Ohio, where she serves as Associate Editor of *Wide Angle,* a film journal. Her prose, poems, and performance pieces have appeared in small-press, national, and international magazines. Her sound poems have been featured in the inaugural edition of *Best American Experimental Writing,* edited by Cole Swensen (Omnidawn, 2014). An educator, Holm works with others in higher education to implement the Americans with Disabilities Act.

SHUBHANGI JOSHI is a poet and musician based in Mumbai, India. She is the author of the poetry collection *To Stir Up an Ornate Nest* (Authorspress, 2014) and the winner of the Commendation Prize at the All India Poetry Competition 2014, organized by the Poetry Society of India. Her poetry has appeared in *Manushi, The Brown Critique, The Voices Project, Levure Littéraire,* and other journals. Joshi originally began writing poetry at the age of sixteen, and over time her writing began to focus on critiquing and challenging Indian societal norms. Having observed first-hand the various ways in which patriarchy manifests itself in Indian society, she felt the need to express her dissent through her music and poetry. Joshi has spoken out against many ills plaguing Indian society, such as domestic violence and female feticide, as well as everyday sexism, in the hope that encouraging discussion on such topics will help end these practices.

JUDY JUANITA's first novel, *Virgin Soul*, was published by Viking Press in 2013. Her poetry and fiction have appeared in *13th Moon, Poetry Monthly, LIPS, Painted Bride Quarterly, Crab Orchard Review, Croton Review* and *Obsidian II*. Also a skilled playwright, Juanita's plays have been produced in the San Francisco Bay Area, Los Angeles, and New York City. Her collection of short stories, *The High Price of Freeways*, was a two-time finalist in the Livingston Press Tartts First Fiction contest in 2014. Juanita earned an MFA in creative writing from San Francisco State University and has taught writing at Laney College since 1993. She believes that vulnerability, dependence/independence and hope/despair can bring about some of the most powerful poetry, drama and fiction.

CINDY E. KING writes to bring insight and understanding to issues related to gender and illness. Her work appeared or is forthcoming in *Callaloo, North American Review, River Styx, Black Warrior Review, American Literary Review, Jubilat, Barrow Street, African American Review*, and elsewhere. Her poems can also be heard online at Weekend America (an American Public Media production), *RHINO Poetry*, and *Bellingham Review*. In 2014, King was awarded a Tennessee Williams Scholarship to attend the Sewanee Writers' Conference. Her book-length poetry manuscript was a finalist for the *Crab Orchard Review* and *Permafrost* First Book Prizes last year. She has also received scholarships and fellowships to attend the New York Summer Writers Institute, the Wesleyan University Writers Conference, the Colgate Writers' Conference, and others. Originally from Cleveland, Ohio, King currently lives in Texas, where she is an Assistant Professor at the University of North Texas at Dallas.

TRICIA KNOLL is a poet from Portland, Oregon. She has degrees in literature from Stanford University (BA) and Yale University (MAT). She began seriously writing poetry in 2007 when, on her first day of retirement from a job in communications with the City of Portland, she started rereading *Leaves of Grass.* In 2011, a potentially life-threatening health challenge (multiple pulmonary embolisms) made her realize she had no time to waste. Knoll also suffers from spasmodic dysphonia, a voice disability that has taught her to listen where once she might have talked. Over one hundred of Knoll's poems have appeared in journals and anthologies, and her poetry chapbook *Urban Wild* was published in 2014 by Finishing Line Press. Knoll is currently working on a collection of poems about the wisdom and perils of aging.

Before her mother and father were diagnosed with late stage cancers in 2010, KAREN LAND worked as a professional dog musher, public speaker, and writer of outdoor columns and features for newspapers and magazines. Land lived in Montana for over fifteen years, but after her mother was diagnosed with uterine carcinosarcoma, she moved back to her childhood home in Indianapolis. Land has given over 1,000 talks in twenty-six states over the past fifteen years, and continued speaking about the wilderness, dog mushing, and the Iditarod Sled Dog Race in schools and libraries until her parents needed full-time care. After fifty years of marriage, Jack and Janice Land passed away in 2012, just five months apart. Land is currently writing a memoir about caregiving and endurance—the beauty and challenges of living together, and dying alone.

JENNIFER MACBAIN-STEPHENS was inspired to write "In the Pink" after watching Léa Pool's documentary *Pink Ribbons, Inc.* (National Film Board of Canada, 2011). Jennifer attended New York University and currently lives in the Washington, D.C., area with her family. She is the author of three poetry chapbooks: *Every Her Dies* (ELJ Publications, 2014), *Clotheshorse* (Finishing Line Press, 2014), and *Backyard Poems* (Dancing Girl Press, forthcoming 2015). Recent work can be seen or is forthcoming in *Toad Suck Review*, *The Poetry Storehouse*, *Pretty Owl Poetry*, *Yes, Poetry*, *Gargoyle Magazine*, *Jet Fuel Review*, and *Hobart*.

JULIA OLDER has lived in France, Italy, Mexico and Brazil. Her published books include *Endometriosis* (Scribners, 1984-2006), *Appalachian Odyssey* (Authors Guild, 2009 reprint; Open Road, 2016 ebook), *Blues for a Black Cat* (University of Nebraska Press, 2001), *Boris Vian Invents Boris Vian* (Black Widow Press, 2015), and two historical novels of her *Isles of Shoals* Trilogy (Appledore Books, 1994 and 2006). Older's eleven poetry titles include the bio-novel *Tahirih Unveiled* (Turning Point, 2007) and *Tales Of The François Vase* (Hobblebush Books, 2012), a book-length poem and verse play on CD. She has received fellowships to the Iowa Workshop, Yaddo, and The MacDowell Colony, a University of Michigan First Hopwood Award, and Puffin, Deming, and NEA Writing Grants. Her work has appeared in *Poets & Writers*, *The New Yorker*, *Entelechy*

International, Nonbinary Review Online, and numerous other publications. She writes full-time in the foothills of Grand Monadnock, New Hampshire.

At age seven ERICA STERNIN began her writing career, making "shape poems" in the style of E.E. Cummings. Shortly after her fiftieth birthday, she was diagnosed with Stage III breast cancer and thyroid cancer. Aware of the research regarding expressive writing and healing, Sternin focused on "writing to heal" alongside her conventional treatment. She has published poetry through the King County Metro Transit *Poetry on Buses* project and in the literary journal *Between the Lines*, as well as on several online venues. Sternin is a trained SoulCollage© facilitator and a children's librarian in Seattle, Washington.

STEPHANIE WAXMAN's work has appeared in dozens of journals and magazines, including *The Missouri Review, The Bitter Oleander, North Dakota Quarterly,* and *West.* Her story "Perfection" was nominated for a Pushcart Prize, and her story "Delicate Touch" is included in the anthology *New Sudden Fiction* (W.W. Norton & Company, 2007). She is also the author of a novel, *Divided Loyalties* (Marco Press, 2010), and a collection of short stories, *Sex and Death* (Marco Press, 2011). Her nonfiction work includes *Muse in the Classroom* (Marco Press, 2014), *Growing Up Feeling Good* (Panjandrum, 1979), *A Helping Handbook – When A Loved One Is Critically Ill* (Marco Press, 2011), and the internationally published *What Is A Girl? What Is A Boy?* (Marco Press, 2010). Waxman currently teaches writing in Los Angeles, where she lives with her husband, Dennis. It was her mother's physical decline that moved Waxman to write "The Outing."

GINA WILLIAMS is a Pacific Northwest native originally from Whidbey Island, Washington. Much of her creative work is influenced by experience and observation. Over the years, she has worked as a firefighter, reporter, housekeeper, caregiver, veterinarian's assistant, tree planter, gas station attendant, technical writer, cocktail waitress, and berry picker. Her most rewarding job has been raising her sons. Williams earned a BA in Journalism/English and an MA in Communications from the University of Oregon. Her writing and visual art have been featured most recently in *Carve*, *The Sun*, *Fugue*, *Palooka*, *Great Weather for Media*, *theNewerYork*, Black Box Gallery, and Gallery 360, among others. She enjoys writing about topics such as gender, illness, aging and class as a way to help herself—and hopefully readers—better understand our oftentimes difficult human condition.

YUAN CHANGMING, eight-time Pushcart nominee and author of four chapbooks (including *Mindscaping*, published by Fowlpox Press in 2014), is probably the world's most widely published poet who speaks Mandarin but writes in English. Growing up in a remote village, Yuan began to learn the English alphabet at nineteen and published several monographs on Chinese-English translation before leaving China. Since mid-2005, Yuan has had poetry appearing in literary publications across thirty-one countries, including *Best Canadian Poetry*, *Best New Poems Online*, *Cincinnati Review* and *Threepenny Review*. He has written (and published) dozens of poems about illness simply because he seems to have a family curse of chronic pain and illness. In particular, his younger son, also a poet, began to suffer from a disc problem eight years ago, which has cost their family huge amounts of time, money and energy. With a

PhD in English from the University of Saskatchewan, Yuan currently tutors and co-edits *Poetry Pacific* with Allen Qing Yuan in Vancouver, British Columbia.

Lifelong comics artist and fiction writer ADELE MOSS is the 2016 interfaith chaplaincy fellow at Colorado College, a former doula for Illinois' first freestanding birth center, and an expert in medieval funerary puppetry. She finds struggle and sweetness in the integration of diverse passions, working with language, ritual, images, objects, and bodies to grasp at the transitions between life and death. A graduate of 826 Valencia's Writing and Publishing Apprenticeship, Moss has won awards for her short fiction and her thesis in Art History. Her prose has appeared in several literary journals and magazines. Installments of her self-published graphic novel are sold in bookstores across the country.

.

Editors

MEGAN WINKELMAN's research and advocacy has focused on mental health stigma, patient narratives, and low-literacy populations, thanks to the support of the Dalai Lama Fellows Program, the Westly Foundation, and the Bay Area Inspire Award. After graduating from Stanford University with a BA in Human Biology, Honors in Feminist Studies, and an MA in Modern Thought and Literature, she moved to London and helped launch the It Gets Brighter Campaign, which collects and features video messages of hope from those living with mental illness. Winkelman is now a member of the University of California, San Francisco, School of Medicine's Class of 2020.

HAYLEY BECKETT works at the Experimental Education Unit at the University of Washington, an inclusive education setting for children with and without physical and developmental disabilities. An aspiring social worker, Beckett cares deeply about pushing back against the stigma of mental health and disability to ensure that all families' physical and emotional needs are met. She has also researched the impact that creating public art can have on individual and community health outcomes in the aftermath of trauma, and believes deeply in the healing power of creative expression. Beckett is a graduate of Whitman College.

MEGAN COLLINS is a graduate of the University of California, Berkeley, where she studied history and education. She currently works at UC Berkeley's Institute for Research on Labor and Employment. Collins's experiences with aging and illness in her family have taught her the importance of positivity and humor as imposed treatment regimens, self-love as a wellness practice, and the incredible resilience required of caretakers in the most difficult moments of life and death.

LIAT LITWIN's interest in health narratives derives from experiences with members of her immediate family, who have shown her the inner workings of the medical field from the perspective of both health care providers and patients. Litwin graduated from Tufts University with a BS in Cognitive and Brain Science, and is especially passionate about exploring the intersection of health and technology in clinical settings. She has worked as a research coordinator investigating virtual reality as a non-pharmacological analgesic for children with sickle cell disease, and at a startup creating digital health tools to empower patients at home. In 2016, Litwin joined the class of 2020 at Sackler School of Medicine in Tel Aviv.

Acknowledgments

Some really talented and wonderful people supported us throughout the process of founding *Uprooted* and creating this print edition. Giulia Meador designed the book's cover and provided invaluable feedback on design and layout decisions. Adele Moss offered her editorial insights and gifted us with a beautifully introspective foreword to introduce both us and the book. Professor Valerie Miner of Stanford University served as the judge of our first-place submission, and Stanford School of Medicine's Professor Audrey Shafer advised our poetry selection process. Adam Creasman offered assistance both tangible and intangible at critical phases of the project's evolution. Mariko Creasman and the Involuntarily Committed Forever Book Club road-tested our discussion questions.

It was only with the support of these and many other people that this book came to fruition. We sincerely thank you.

...

The *Uprooted* project is more than just this book—it also exists online. You can find more illness and gender narratives and learn how to contribute at www.uprootedanthology.com.

Notes

Bidart, Frank. "Ellen West," *In the Western Night: Collected Poems, 1965-90*. New York: Farrar Straus Giroux, 1990. Accessed via poetryfoundation.org. (Appears in "Hospital Poems" by Sarah Feldman.)

Hoffman, Diane E., and Anita J. Tarzian. "The Girl Who Cried Pain: A Bias Against Women in the Treatment of Pain," *Journal of Law, Medicine & Ethics*, 2001 (Vol. 29, pp. 13-27). Accessed online via ssrn.com. (Appears in "Tender Points" by Amy Berkowitz.)

Miller, Arthur. *Death of a Salesman*, 1986. New York: Penguin Books. (Appears in "How to Be a Wife" by Cathleen Calbert.)

Miller, Jenni. "'Punk Singer' Kathleen Hanna on Riot Grrrls Grown Up," *Film.com*, 2 Dec. 2013. Web. (Appears in "Tender Points" by Amy Berkowitz.)

Morris, David B. *The Culture of Pain*, 1991. Berkeley: UC Press. (Appears in "Tender Points" by Amy Berkowitz.)

National Institutes of Health. "Questions and Answers about Fibromyalgia," 2015. Accessed online via niams.nih.gov. (Appears in "Tender Points" by Amy Berkowitz.)

The Troggs. *Love Is All Around*, Larry Page, 1967. MP3. (Appears in "How to Be a Wife" by Cathleen Calbert.)

Wordsworth, William. *Resolution and Independence*, J. Lane, 1904. (Appears in "How to Be a Wife" by Cathleen Calbert.)

www.ingramcontent.com/pod-product-compliance
Lightning Source LLC
LaVergne TN
LVHW041216080426
835508LV00011B/970